PLEASING GOD

PLEASING GOD

by

David L. Hocking

Published by
HERE'S LIFE PUBLISHERS, INC.
San Bernardino, California 92402

PLEASING GOD

by David L. Hocking

Published by
HERE'S LIFE PUBLISHERS, INC.
P. O. Box 1576
San Bernardino, CA 92402

Library of Congress Catalogue Card 84-047802
ISBN 0-89840-065-1
HLP Product No. 950774
© 1984, Here's Life Publishers, Inc.

Printed in the United States of America.

Unless otherwise indicated, Scripture quotations are from the New American Standard Bible, © the Lockman Foundation 1960, 1962, 1963, 1971, 1972, 1973, 1975, and are used by permission.

Table of Contents

FOREWORD

WITHIN THE HEART of every man there is a unique capacity for God. That is what makes us different from the animals. We have an intuitive desire to please God.

Unfortunately, we also have a desire to please ourselves. And we cannot do both until we surrender our will to God's in a sincere quest to please Him. Then, pleasing God becomes synonymous with pleasing ourselves. That is when we experience the ultimate in inner peace.

As Paul said, "Let the peace of God rule in your hearts" (Colossians 3:14) by doing everything to please and glorify God (verses 16 and 17).

But how can we please God? Does it require prayer and fasting, self-imposed celibacy, asceticism or other forms of self-denial? Do we please God by drawing up a legal list of things we do not do? The Bible has much to say about man pleasing God—and the amazing thing is, it enriches man's life when he does so.

This book will help you understand how to

please God.

Most people don't know how. The unsaved don't know and don't care. But Christians who don't know how to please God feel unfulfilled. Actually, it isn't all that difficult to please God if you (1) are willing, and (2) know how.

Dave Hocking has a sincere desire to please God in his own personal life, and he desires to help others learn how. The only way to teach that is to examine what the Bible says on the subject. Pastor. Hocking is a master at that. Everything he teaches, whether publicly or in print, is Bible-based.

Reading this book will help you learn to apply basic biblical principles to your everyday Christian life and it will enable you to enjoy the "peace" that follows pleasing God.

Dr. Tim LaHaye, President
Family Life Seminars

INTRODUCTION

A MIDDLE-AGED COUPLE were looking at a new car in the dealer's showroom. The man said, "I like it." He looked at it some more and said, "I *really* like it." Finally, sitting behind the wheel, he looked at his wife with the expression of a little boy and said, "I want it!" It was a TV commercial.

Then the music crescendoed and the message was sung loud and clear: "You can have it!" (Of course, there's a small matter of financing, but that can easily be worked out.)

The approach of that commercial capitalizes on a cultural understanding of our day—if you want it, you can have it. The message centers in *pleasing yourself*. Why not? You deserve it. You're worth it.

We are being told to "go for it," "grab all the gusto" we can get. We're given the impression that if we don't do it now, we may never do it at all. So, today's ubiquitous advertising hype produces dissatisfaction in our hearts over what we now have. It makes us want something else because of the pleasure we will derive from it or the benefit it will be to our self esteem, our sense of worth. How much money does one need to be happy? The answer is *"More."*

But, let's stop and ask, where is this *selfism*, this hedonism, leading us? Is it helping us overcome the problems of crime, alcoholism, drug abuse, divorce, loneliness, and so on? What does the pursuit of pleasure do to our sense of duty, morality, and responsibility?

Is the only goal in life "doing your own thing," or "getting to know yourself?" Are we the masters of our own fate, the controllers of our destiny? Where does God fit in?

No doubt about it—selfism is a doctrine implicit in modern culture. It's the consumer philosophy *par excellence*. It attracts those with money and leisure. I find that "to please myself" comes naturally. It's not hard to accept the ideas of those who tell me how great I am and how I deserve much more than I have so far obtained in life.

But inside, such thinking doesn't produce the desired result. Instead of being satisfied, the thirst for *more* produces restlessness and emotional turmoil. Acquiring the "goodies" does not bring peace of mind and meaning to my life. Something more is needed.

The focus today is man, not God. That's our problem. The Bible teaches that we were not designed to please ourselves. We were created to glorify the God who made us. What does God want us to do? He wants us to honor and praise Him in all we do and say. So we need to get our eyes off ourselves, and onto the plan of God. The peace, joy, love, and purpose in life that all of us desire are to be found in the pursuit of God, not in self-enhancement or self-aggrandizement.

But that raises some questions. How do we please God? What can we do to change the focus of our lives from self to Him? What are we doing now that hinders our ability to please Him? What differences can we expect to find once we start trying to do that?

This book is an attempt to help you get started. It will help me as well, as I try to expose the problems that confront us all. At times I will come down hard on secular views, ideas that you may have accepted already without much thought or analysis. I will present biblical proof. My goal is to help us think and act in conformity to what God desires for every one of us.

At the end of each chapter, I include a section called "A Place to Begin." In it I will try to relate what the Bible says to our real life in this late twentieth century. We will look together for insights and practical principles that will change our focus from self to God. The results may border on the revolutionary. Our lives will become more meaningful. We will discover new purposes, a deepening spiritual reality. It's possible that what you read here will set you free to be all that God designed you to be.

One thing is sure. This book will get us to focus on God—looking for His perspective on who we are, why we are here, and what He expects from us.

Chapter 1

Why Please God?

WHEN I WAS A student, I was always asking *why*. Sometimes I never found out. And I'm not all that different today. But I can usually respond better to something when I know the reason behind it. When I know why I should do something, it helps me get started. If the reasons make sense, they usually motivate me.

Since my natural tendency is to please myself, I need to be reminded often why I should please God. Maybe you feel the same.

One beautiful summer evening in the mountains above San Bernardino, California, a friend and I were sitting on a huge rock looking at the stars. It seemed as if the sky was especially brilliant with the light of those stars. The smell of pine trees, the crisp freshness of the mountain air, the quietness— all still linger in my memory. Our thoughts turned to the One who created the beauty and majesty of the physical universe. My friend said, "Just think— God created all this to please Himself."

The Purpose of Creation

Creation gives us a reason to please God. Everything God made was designed to bring Him pleasure, and that includes you and me.

The twenty-four elders pictured in heaven in the last book of the Bible fell down before God on His throne and worshiped Him saying: "Worthy art Thou, our Lord and our God, to receive glory and honor and power; for Thou didst create all things, and because of Thy will they existed, and were created" (Rev. 4:11). The King James Version renders that last phrase, "and for Thy pleasure they are and were created." All things were created because of the *will* and *pleasure* of God. He created us to glorify and worship Him. He is the Creator; we are the created. That should be reason enough for us to try to please Him in everything.

"The earth is the LORD'S and all it contains, The world and those who dwell in it" (Ps. 24:1). Creation by God means that we belong to Him and should fulfill His purposes. Psalm 19:1 states: "The heavens are telling of the glory of God." Psalm 8:1 exclaims, "O LORD, our LORD, How majestic is Thy name in all the earth, Who hast displayed Thy splendor above the heavens!"

God knows the purpose of all things. It was never His desire to see His creation honor itself. When the people He created seek to please themselves, they are doing what is foreign to their original design. It results in destructive behavior.

For the wrath of God is revealed from heaven

against all ungodliness and unrighteousness of men, who suppress the truth in unrighteousness, because that which is known about God is evident within them; for God made it evident to them. For since the creation of the world His invisible attributes, His eternal power and divine nature, have been clearly seen, being understood through what has been made, so that they are without excuse. For even though they knew God, they did not honor Him as God, or give thanks; but they became futile in their speculations, and their foolish heart was darkened. Professing to be wise, they became fools, and exchanged the glory of the incorruptible man and of birds and four-footed animals and crawling creatures. There God gave them over in the lusts of their hearts to impurity, that their bodies might be dishonored among them. For they exchanged the truth of God for a lie, and worshiped and served the creature rather than the Creator, who is blessed forever. Amen (Rom. 1:18-25).

Worshiping and serving the creature rather than the Creator—there's the problem. That's the issue behind our present culture's selfism. It is worship of the created, instead of the Creator.

Such a philosophy cannot succeed. Its tenets may look good on the surface, but they lack depth. Its pleasure and happiness are short-lived, unfulfilling.

The Sovereignty of God

In our day, God's sovereignty is rarely recognized, much less honored. Man-centered theology limits God's involvement and control. It believes that God has left many things in our hands, even that He depends more on human beings than on His

15

own intervention. Nor is the problem resolved by our merely affirming that we believe in God's sovereignty. The fact is, our perspective is largely governed by our own experiences. We don't see things from God's viewpoint. We often find it hard to visualize His presence in the affairs of human life. We even frequently doubt that our concerns have come to His attention. In some circles, the idea of human responsibility has taken over as the essence of Christian theology. God's sovereignty is thought to be the doctrine of a few socially unconcerned and apathetic nonintellectuals whose views rarely demonstrate any relevance to contemporary problems and issues.

In contrast to that humanistic reasoning, the psalmist declares: "But our God is in the heavens; He does whatever He pleases" (Ps. 115:3). The Psalms point to God's sovereignty, His involvement, in the processes of nature: "For I know that the LORD is great, And that our LORD is above all Gods. Whatever the LORD pleases, He does, In heaven and in earth, in the seas and in all deeps. He causes the vapors to ascend from the ends of the earth; Who makes lightnings for the rain; Who brings forth the wind from His treasuries" (Ps. 135:5-7).

Psalm 147:5 says, "Great is our LORD, and abundant in strength; His understanding is infinite." After declaring His greatness, it goes on to specify how that truth affects our lives. For example, the Lord:

verse 6 — "supports the afflicted"
verse 8 — "covers the heavens with clouds"
"provides rain for the earth"
"makes grass to grow on the mountains"

16

verse 9 — "gives to the beast its food,
   And to the young ravens which cry"
verse 14 — "satisfies you with the finest of the
   wheat"
verse 16 — "gives snow like wool"
   "scatters the hoar-frost like ashes"
verse 18 — "causes His wind to blow and the
   waters to flow"

God's sovereignty is constantly evident in nature and in human life.

The Example of Jesus Christ

If we needed a further reason to please God in all we think, say, and do, we have the example of Jesus Christ. Jesus said, "I always do the things that are pleasing to Him" (Jn 8:29). Always? That's what He said. Our Lord's constant desire was to please His Father in heaven. Christians who want to be Christlike in all they do should therefore seek to please God in everything. No exceptions. "Now we who are strong ought to bear the weaknesses of those without strength and not just please ourselves. Let each of us please his neighbor for his good, to his edification. For even Christ did not please Himself; but as it is written, 'The reproaches of those who reproached Thee fell upon Me'" (Rom. 15:1-3).

The life of our Lord was centered in others, not in Himself. He came to seek and to save the lost (Lk. 19:10), not to live for His own pleasure. The apostle John said that "He laid down His life for us" (1 Jn. 3:16) and "we ought to lay down our lives for the brethren."

The spirit of sacrifice is obviously not one of the

17

tenets of hedonism. When life is filled with the pursuit of pleasure, there are few thoughts of duty.

If I am following Christ, then my goal, too, should be to relate to others and serve them, not to please myself. Now, I don't have any ability to control my "old self" (my sin nature) when it comes to wanting to please myself. If you ask me, "Where would you like to serve as a missionary?" I'd probably choose Hawaii or Tahiti. I like those places. But there are some places I wouldn't choose. The question is, do we always somehow manage to go where we want to go?

"Delight yourself in the LORD; and He will give you the desires of your heart" (Ps. 37:4). Let me tell you, the "desires of your heart" are based on whether or not you are making the Lord the joy of your life. He can change those desires and make you happy wherever you are, even if when you started you weren't pleased with it. If none of us went to places and did things we didn't like, how much of the world would be evangelized? How many missionaries would go to the majority of peoples today who have never heard the gospel of Christ if their going was entirely based on whether or not it really pleased them to do that?

Our Accountability to God

Not only the example of Christ, but also my own accountability to God causes me to say I am to please God and not myself. The apostle Paul wrote these marvelous words about himself and the future: "We are of good courage, I say, and prefer rather to be absent from the body and to be at home with the Lord" (2 Cor. 5:8). Those are precious words. Many years ago when my father died, we had a giant plaque placed in the inside lid of his casket: "Absent from the body, present with the Lord." We wanted everyone to know that he wasn't dead; he was with Christ. That is a wonderful statement: to know that if I die I'm going to be with Jesus Christ. To know that relieves me of many hassles, pressures, and burdens. Then Paul went on to say: "Therefore also we have as our ambition, whether at home or absent, to be pleasing to Him" (v. 9).

Why? "For we must all appear before the judgment seat of Christ, that each one may be recompensed for his deeds in the body, according to what he has done, whether good or bad" (v. 10).

We are accountable to God. The fact that I will stand before Him is a motivating factor for me to please God rather than myself.

The Testimony of Paul

In the book of Galatians, the apostle Paul specifically discussed his ministry as it related to pleasing God. He talked about not preaching a different gospel, warning those Galatians not to listen to something that wasn't the truth. Then he said: "For am I now seeking the favor of men, or of God? Or am I striving to please men? If I were still trying to please men, I would not be a bond-servant of Christ" (Gal. 1:10).

Paul continually used one title about himself, *doulos*, which means a bondslave of Jesus Christ. He said, in effect, "If you're trying to please human beings rather than God, you're not a bondslave to Christ."

19

Now behind those words of Paul is a story. I believe that the Galatian letter was written to the churches of Antioch in Pisidia, Iconium, Lystra, and Derbe. (That's my view. If you read various commentators, you'll find there are several views.) In my opinion, this letter was written to the churches of Paul's first missionary journey. When he went on that first journey, he left Antioch in Syria and went to the island of Cyprus where he ministered with Barnabas. They went from there to a region called Pamphylia, which is the southern part of Turkey, its lowlands or marshlands.

Following this, according to Paul's letters, something happened in Perga that caused him a physical affliction. Some say it was an eye disease that created a festering condition, a horrible thing to look at. Paul spoke of having problems with his eyes (Gal. 4:13-15; 6:11). He said, too, that his bodily illness brought him to them (4:13). It may be that he had speech difficulties as well—which hardly puts him in our categories of an ideal Christian leader! I suspect he was short; the name *Paul* means "little." In our churches he might not have been seen over most of the pulpits. Yet this man almost turned the world upside down. We should be careful, shouldn't we, how we evaluate the qualities and essentials of leadership.

As to the reason Paul went up to the higher elevations of Antioch, Iconium, Lystra, and Derbe, it may be that the lowlands had much disease. So Paul, already sickly, went to the highlands, where God blessed him and gave him great ministry.

Beyond those physical problems, Paul suffered

a lot of persecution. He wrote about that in several of his epistles (for example, 2 Cor. 11:23-28). He was stoned and left for dead in Lystra. He had gone through tremendous punishment before the time when he wrote to these people and said, "You're attacking me because people have persuaded you not to accept my confrontation of a false gospel. You're attacking me as though somehow I have wrong motives. What are they? If I were trying to please human beings and gain their favor, I wouldn't be a bondslave of Christ. Nor would I have done what I did when I was with you." That's the whole point of the argument.

Let's translate this into our experience. He means that pleasing God will sometimes bring to a person's life things that are not too pleasant. Beyond that, he was saying that certain trials and difficulties have a way of purifying our motives regarding why we're doing what we're doing. If my reasons for my actions are not based on my strong desire to please God, I will not easily endure. If my desire is not to hear, "Well done, good and faithful servant; . . . enter thou into the joy of thy Lord" (KJV) why go on? Why not just quit and throw in the towel?

At several points in my ministry, I have felt ready to quit. One particular time I remember very well. It was a Monday morning and I wanted to give up, but God had an encouragement in store for me.

A good friend was traveling through Kansas, when he saw something that I needed to see. It seems that a pastor in one of the small Kansas towns also had been feeling that he just couldn't take it anymore. He was very much loved by the people in his church, and this news stirred them to action.

21

They made a gigantic banner and tied it between two trees where everyone could see it when driving through. It read, "PASTOR, DON'T QUIT!"

My friend stopped and took a picture of that banner and sent it to me. It arrived on that Monday morning, and I still have it.

Sure, we get tired in the ministry, and sometimes we want to give up. But the Bible says, "And let us not lose heart in doing good, for in due time, we shall reap if we do not grow weary" (Gal. 6:9).

Do you know why a lot of people don't keep going? It's because they have their eyes on other people and not on God. We are concerned with what they think of us. The pressure and guilt can be enormous, more than we feel we can carry. So we must learn to please God. Paul said, "If I was seeking to please men, then explain what happened to me in the Galatian churches. Why did I spend day after day confronting people who disagreed with my message, argued with me, stoned, and persecuted me? Explain it. Why would I want that? There can be only one reason and that is because I was seeking to please God, not people."

In another letter Paul wrote: "Slaves, in all things obey those who are your masters on earth, not with external service, as those who merely please men, but with sincerity of heart, fearing the Lord. Whatever you do, do your work heartily, as for the Lord, rather than for men" (Col. 3:22-23).

Even in the instruction to slaves, we learn that one's highest goal in life should be to please God. Now slaves were programmed to please men. They could never question the will of their masters. According to Roman law, rebellion would result in death. Masters could break families, using slaves in any manner they wished. They could misuse them, abuse them, and not be held accountable for it as long as they provided food, clothing, and housing for them. "Slaves," Paul wrote, "don't just please men, please the Lord. Do your work heartily as to the Lord." As a slave, imagine becoming a Christian and hearing Paul say that. "Work with all your might. Work more than you've ever worked before so your masters have no reason to question your claim of believing in the Lord." What a statement!

The Results of Selfism

Now let's look at the results of pleasing self. "For the mind set on the flesh is death, but the mind set on the Spirit is life and peace, because the mind set on the flesh is hostile toward God; for it does not subject itself to the law of God, for it is not even able to do so, and those who are in the flesh cannot please God" (Rom. 8:6-8).

Allowing self—that is, our sin nature—to be pleased, pampered, coddled, and stroked means we cannot please God. To be selfish means we are consumed with our own needs. In that state of mind, we easily doubt that God cares.

Do you sometimes think God is ignoring you? Do you think He doesn't really love you? That He doesn't even know what you need? That He may leave you helpless, alone, forsaken, isolated? The Bible says that God knows what we need before we ask Him (Mt. 6:32). He loves us and cares about us more than anyone does here on this earth.

Our generation is so programmed toward "getting our needs met" that we've lost sight of how that really happens. God is fully capable of meeting each and every need. He wants our happiness more than we do. He wants to bless us more than we want to receive His blessing.

I remember the joy I felt when I first realized this. I finally understood that God was not trying to beat me. He was not waiting for me to sin so he could bash me around and cause me to shape up. God is in love with me and with you. Through Christ He is blessing us every day with "every spiritual blessing in the heavenly places in Christ" (Eph. 1:3).

Hebrews 13:20, 21 states: "Now the God of peace, who brought up from the dead the great Shepherd of the sheep through the blood of the eternal covenant, even Jesus our Lord, equip you in every good thing to do His will, working in us that which is pleasing in His sight, through Jesus Christ, to whom be the glory forever and ever." According to this text, God's will, which He is working in me and equipping me to do, is bringing about what is pleasing in His sight.

A Place to Begin

We have yet to explore specific ways in which we can please God, and the remaining chapters of this book are dedicated to that end. The thing to get settled at this point is your basic commitment. Is it to please God, or is it to please yourself? *Now is a time to think this matter over and decide.*

Knowing the reasons I should please God will help motivate me, but knowing *why* doesn't mean that pleasing God has become my motive. I don't always know what my motives are. Often I am confused about them until I actually do what God tells me to do and then look back and evaluate what I've done in light of what the Bible teaches. That helps.

My natural tendency, as I have said, is to please myself, not God. I know that I should please Him, but I don't always do it. So it helps me to review the purposes behind my goal of pleasing and glorifying God. When I question something that I plan to do—as to whether it accomplishes the goal of pleasing God—it helps me to analyze it in light of why I should please God. Because I know I'm accountable to God, that recollection sometimes checks my plans. It stops me from doing something I shouldn't do.

I find it necessary to renew my commitment to God frequently. It helps me to pray these words:

"Lord, I know You desire me to please You in all I say and do. I not only believe in You and love You, but I once again commit myself, my time, my abilities, my possessions—all that I am and have—to You. I desire to please You always, and I need Your power and strength to do it."

Before you read any further, why not make this commitment to God? Pray right now and dedicate yourself and all that you have to the ultimate objective: pleasing God alone.

Chapter 2

Who Gets the Glory?

YEARS AGO WHEN I played basketball, we had a name for players who shot the ball every time they got their hands on it. They were "glory hounds." Some players can't relate to other members of the team because already they see their names in the headlines of tomorrow's paper. They want all the glory.

So who gets the glory in your life? Tough question. We often don't face the fact that we have a natural tendency to desire personal fame and importance to the neglect of weightier issues. We prefer to think of ourselves as humble rather than egotistically wanting to be first. We like others to relate to us as though we are significant in their lives. Sometimes we are amazed that others are able to cope with life's problems without our help. We have a "glory" problem.

The ancient Corinthians also had a glory problem. Representing the finest of Greek culture and learning, they were proud of their achievements. Corinthian architecture was ornate and decorative, revealing the flair that these people had for life and the pursuit of pleasure. Even among the Corinthian Christians, that hedonistic lifestyle and intellectual arrogance were combined with problems of factionalism, alcoholism, immorality, divorce, abuse of spiritual gifts, and the absence of love for others. To this Corinthian church Paul wrote: "Whether, then, you eat or drink or whatever you do, do all to the glory of God" (1 Cor. 10:31). Quoting the Old Testament book of Jeremiah, he also said to them: "Let him who boasts, boast in the LORD" (1 Cor. 1:31).

The Corinthian culture was dominated by selfish pursuits and an intense desire to glory in human achievements. The Christians there were seeking to please themselves, not God. That's our problem too. We are encouraged to be like that by the society in which we live. "After all, if you don't take care of yourself, who will?" The Bible, on the other hand, teaches a very important principle: "Whether, then, you eat or drink or whatever you do, do all to the glory of God" (1 Cor. 10:31).

A remarkable commentary on God's desires for us is found in the writings of the prophet Jeremiah: "Thus says the LORD, 'Let not a wise man boast of his wisdom, and let not the mighty man boast of his might, let not a rich man boast of his riches; but let him who boasts boast of this, that he understands and knows Me, that I am the LORD who exercises lovingkindness, justice, and righteousness on earth; for I delight in these things,' declares the LORD" (Jer. 9:23-24).

Why do we boast so much? Why do we take credit in large and small matters instead of giving the glory and praise to God?

Who Should Get The Glory?

According to the Bible, Jesus should get the glory in our lives. He is to be number one. If we are going to please God in our lives, we must learn to exalt and honor God's Son. "Therefore also God highly exalted Him, and bestowed on Him the name which is above every name, that at the name of Jesus every knee should bow, of those who are in heaven, and on earth, and under the earth, and that every tongue should confess that Jesus Christ is Lord, to the glory of God the Father" (Phil. 2:9-11).

God the Father is glorified when His Son is exalted. Jesus said, "He who does not honor the Son does not honor the Father Who sent Him" (Jn. 5:23).

Why Should We Glorify Jesus Christ?

Several years ago in a seminar for pastors, I was speaking on some objectives that every church should have as their philosophy of ministry. The first objective I mentioned was the worship and praise of God the Father and His Son, Jesus Christ our Lord. It was quite revealing to hear from these pastors (over 100 of them) that not one of their churches had included this objective in their constitutions or policy statements.

Matters like evangelism and the edification of believers were the objectives most often stated by these churches. But the worship of God was somehow ignored or neglected. That tells us something about what is wrong in our churches today.

After I had preached on the subject of worship one Sunday morning, a woman came up to me and said, "I have such a desire to learn how to worship the Lord. For many years I have come to church expecting to receive a blessing from the Lord and have my needs ministered to. I see now that my priorities are not straight. I have left out the worship and praise of God. I should come to church each week with a conscious desire to worship my Lord."

The results of our narcissistic age have been far less than was promised. Selfism has done little to enrich our church services and minister to the hearts of believers. We are staggering, so to speak, after coming through this period of entertainment-prone, experience-oriented churchianity. Its theology has been weak; its methods have often seemed childish. The quest for success and self-improvement has left a vacuum in our hearts which, I believe, only the worship of God can fill.

There is a great hunger today among Christians to learn how to praise and glorify God. We have been cheated of our spiritual heritage. We need to return to our roots, find our joy in knowing God and rejoice in who He is and in what He can do.

And He [Jesus] is the image of the invisible God, the first-born of all creation. For in Him all things were created, both in the heavens and on earth, visible and invisible, whether thrones or dominions or rulers or authorities—all things have been created through Him and for Him. And He is before all things, and in Him all things hold together. He is also head of the body, the church; and He is the beginning, the first-born from the dead; so that He Himself might come to have first place in everything. For it was the Father's good pleasure for all the fulness to dwell in Him (Col. 1:15-19).

A literal translation of that last sentence, verse 19, would read, "all the fulness [referring to God] was pleased to dwell in Him."

1. *We should glorify Jesus Christ because of His unique personhood.* Jesus was made human like us. But He was divine, and we are not. Although God is able to live in us, Jesus claimed to be God in human flesh. He was both God and man. He was one personality with two natures, human and divine.

That kind of uniqueness should cause us to fall at His feet and worship Him. Concerning His Son, God said, "And let all the angels of God worship Him" (Heb. 1:6).

Jesus is "the image of the invisible God" (Col. 1:15). An image is a copy. It is like seeing your face in the water. Every image is a likeness, but every likeness is not an image. (Two people can look alike but not have the same parents.)

Hebrews 1:3 describes Jesus as "the radiance of His glory and the exact representation of His nature." The words "exact representation" refer in Greek to the imprint of a tool. John 1:18 says, "No man has seen God at any time; the only begotten God, who is in the bosom of the Father, He has explained Him." Some manuscripts of that verse read "only begotten *Son*" and others read "only begotten *God*." Whichever it is, the verse teaches that

Jesus has revealed the unseen God. The Gospel of John adds these amazing words: "Philip said to Him, 'Lord, show us the Father, and it is enough for us.' Jesus said to him, 'Have I been so long with you, and yet you have not come to know Me, Philip? He who has seen Me has seen the Father; how do you say, "Show us the Father"?'" (14:8-9).

Jesus came to reveal to us what God is like. God became a man in order to communicate with us, the creatures He made (Jn. 1:1, 14).

Jesus is not the same as the Father. He displays the Father. Jesus and the Father are the same in nature (both are divine), but they are separate in personality and work. It is not easy to understand. In trying to explain this to a friend, I pointed to some ants crawling on the ground and asked what would be the best way to communicate with those ants. He answered, "Become an ant." "That's what God did when He became a man," I replied. *Incarnation* was the best way to communicate with us. The unique Personhood of Jesus Christ should motivate us to fall at His feet and proclaim, "My Lord and my God" (Jn. 20:28).

2. *We should glorify Jesus Christ because of His preeminence.* To say that Jesus Christ is preeminent over everything and everyone (except His heavenly Father) is reason enough to exalt and worship Him. His preeminence should keep us from praising ourselves, from worshiping ourselves and our own interests.

Jesus is "the first-born of all creation" (Col. 1:15). The word *first-born* is used nine times in the New Testament. In Matthew 1:25 and Luke 2:7 it refers to Jesus as the "first-born son" (KJV) of Mary. It is used in Hebrews 11:28 to refer to the "first-born" who was killed by the death angel if no blood had been put on the lintel and doorposts of the homes of the Egyptians and Israelites.

The word is also used in Hebrews 12:23 to refer to believers in heaven. They are called the "church of the first-born (ones)." This probably refers to the fact that the dead in Christ will rise first (1 Thess. 4:16), before those believers who are alive at the second coming of Christ. Jesus Christ is called "the first-born from the dead (ones)" in Colossians 1:18. He was the first one to rise from the dead without ever experiencing death again. Because He lives, we also shall live. Our resurrection is guaranteed by His resurrection.

The word *first-born* does not necessarily mean first from the standpoint of time. Romans 8:29 refers to God's plan to conform believers to the "image of His Son." His reason for doing this was "that He [Jesus] might be the first-born among many brethren." Believers of Old Testament times were born before Christ was born of Mary. He is the "first-born" in the sense of being special, as in Hebrews 1:6: "And when He again brings the first-born into the world, He says, 'And let all the angels of God worship Him.'"

Jesus is also called the "only begotten" Son of God. The word is used nine times in the New Testament and can refer to the only son or daughter of someone (Lk. 7:12; 8:42; 9:38). But Jesus was not the only son of Joseph and Mary. According to Mark 6:3, there were four more sons and some daughters. When the apostle John used the term he spoke of

Jesus as the "only begotten" Son of God the Father (Jn. 1:14, 18; 3:16, 18; 1 Jn. 4:9).

But God has other sons also. Jesus is not the only Son of God. How do we explain this? The Bible speaks of Isaac as the "only-begotten son" of Abraham: "By faith Abraham, when he was tested, offered up Isaac; and he who had received the promises was offering up his only begotten son; it was he to whom it was said, 'In Isaac your seed shall be called.'" (Heb. 11:17,18). Abraham had other sons. But Isaac was his unique son in that the line of Messiah came through Isaac, not through Ishmael or any of Abraham's other sons. Jesus is the unique Son of God. There is no other son like Him. But all believers are "sons of God," or children of God, by faith in Jesus Christ as Lord and Savior. Jesus, however, is preeminent.

3. *We should glorify Jesus Christ because of His great power.* The New Testament is explicit about the mighty creative power of Jesus Christ: "For in Him all things were created, both in the heavens and on earth, visible and invisible, whether thrones or dominions or rulers or authorities—all things have been created through Him and for Him" (Col. 1:16). The creation of all that is should cause us to bow down and worship the Lord Jesus Christ. "All things came into being through Him; and apart from Him nothing came into being that has come into being" (Jn. 1:3). He is the Creator of the universe and of humankind.

The above verse from Colossians points to three things about that creative power: (1) Its origin—"*in* Him all things were created"; (2) Its operation—"all things have been created *through* Him"; (3) Its object—"and *for* Him." Jesus is the source, channel, and ultimate objective of all things. He had the power to create the material universe out of nothing. He has the power to sustain its laws and its existence. He has the power to cause everything to bring Him glory and praise.

4. *We should glorify Jesus Christ because of His pre-existence.* Before the universe was created and human life began, Jesus was existing. "And He is before all things" (Col. 1:17). He was alive and well long before He was born as a baby in Bethlehem. The Gospel of John pictures Jesus as the Word or, in Greek, the *Logos.* John 1:14 says, "The Word became flesh," which suggests that He was already existing in another form. God is spirit (Jn. 4:24) but when Jesus came into the world, God became flesh (incarnate).

"In the beginning was the Word, and the Word was with God, and the Word was God" (Jn. 1:1). The phrase "in the beginning" (cf. Gen. 1:1) tells us that Jesus was in existence before the worlds were created. Knowledge of His pre-existence should cause us to glorify Him.

The Jews of Jesus' day regarded Abraham as their father. To them Jesus said some remarkable words: "Truly, truly, I say to you, before Abraham was born, I *am*" (Jn. 8:58). He didn't say "before Abraham was born, I *was*," but rather "before Abraham was born, I *am*." He claimed to be living at the time of Abraham, which was over two thousand years preceding this incident. The Jewish leaders were not mistaken about the implications of His statement. They recognized that He was claiming to be the eternal, always existing, God. "Therefore they picked up stones to throw at Him" (Jn. 8:59). Stoning was the penalty for blasphemy.

Was Jesus a blasphemer, a paranoid personality with delusions of grandeur, or is He who He claimed to be: the pre-existent Son of God who created all things?

5. *We should glorify Jesus Christ because of His wonderful providence.* The term *providence* connotes guidance and control. Hebrews 1:3 describes the Son as One who "upholds all things by the word of His power." "In Him all things hold together" (Col. 1:17). All the laws of the universe are being sustained by Jesus' mighty power and loving concern. Nothing is excluded from that providential control.

Psalm 104 speaks of God's marvelous care and control over the forces of nature, of how He provides for both man and beast. "O LORD, how many are Thy works!" the Psalmist wrote, "In wisdom Thou hast made them all; The earth is full of Thy possessions" (v. 24). And, "Let the glory of the LORD endure forever; Let the LORD be glad in His works; He looks at the earth, and it trembles; He touches the mountains, and they smoke. I will sing to the LORD as long as I live; I will sing praise to my God while I have my being. Let my meditation be pleasing to Him; As for me, I shall be glad in the LORD" (vv. 31-34).

And so I ask myself, what kind of praise has come from my mouth in response to my Lord's wonderful providential care for me?

6. *We should glorify Jesus Christ because of His exalted place of authority.* The head of the church is not a pastor, bishop, elder, or pope. It is Jesus

Christ (Col. 1:18). Paul wrote, "And He put all things in subjection under His feet, and gave Him as head over all things to the church, which is His body, the fulness of Him who fills all in all" (Eph. 1:22,23).

This crucial point about the exalted position of Jesus Christ among believers is unfolded in detail in the book of Ephesians: "But speaking the truth in love, we are to grow up in all aspects into Him, who is the *head*, even Christ, from whom the whole body, being fitted and held together by that which every joint supplies, according to the proper working of each individual part, causes the growth of the body for the building up of itself in love" (Eph. 4:15,16).

Jesus' authority in the church is fundamental to the proper functioning of believers with each other. When Jesus is not given His rightful place, then trouble starts. When He is not consulted through prayer and His written Word, we are presuming upon the grace of God. We begin to think that the title *head* is nothing more than an elevated spiritual thought with little practical application.

I remember a terrible business meeting I had many years ago with the members of the church board where I was serving as pastor. We began a serious meeting without prayer. The emotions and outbursts of that evening were far from pleasing to the Lord. We had forgotten a very simple rule: Jesus is the Head and must be recognized as that in all we do. Prayer is one way we demonstrate our belief in the authority of Jesus Christ. Do we consult him in prayer?

God is pleased when we exalt His Son. That means recognizing His place of authority and submitting to Him. Lordship demands obedience. If Jesus is in charge, then His counsel, wisdom, and commands must be followed. To do that is not an option or a creative alternative; it is essential. We glorify God when we submit to the authority of Jesus Christ in the church. We can please God only when this is applied. To believe is to obey.

7. *We should glorify Jesus Christ because of His special position among the believers.* Jesus is "to have first place in everything" (Col. 1:18). God the Father "raised Him from the dead, and seated Him at His right hand in the heavenly places, far above all rule and authority and power and dominion, and every name that is named, not only in this age, but also in the one to come" (Eph. 1:20,21). Paul referred to this special position of Christ a number of times. "If then you have been raised up with Christ, keep seeking the things above, where Christ is, seated at the right hand of God" (Col. 3:1). "Who is the one who condemns? Christ Jesus is He who died, yes, rather who was raised, who is at the right hand of God, who also intercedes for us" (Rom. 8:34).

Jesus' special position as the resurrected Lord is both a reminder and guarantee to all believers of the fact that He is constantly interceding for us and, in some mysterious sense, we are presently seated with Him in the heavenly places. To be seated as a High Priest was not allowed in the service of the tabernacle and the temple. There were no chairs for the priests as they performed their ministry. But our great High Priest "sat down at the right hand of the Majesty on high" (Heb. 1:3). His work has been completed.

The work of redemption has been settled. Jesus' sacrifice for sins was final and sufficient (Heb. 10:11-14). His special position at the right hand of God is a constant testimony to our redemption and the promise of our future resurrection.

To please God we must exalt His Son in our lives. A sure sign that a believer is pleasing himself is when he talks little about Jesus and much about himself. A man named Charles Beatty was an example of this to me. He served on a church staff as associate pastor in charge of evangelism and discipleship ministries. Even though he had little formal education, he was in love with the Lord. It was a rare day when Charles ever spoke of his own needs or his personal problems. It seemed that he really thought about Jesus more than he did about himself. He cared for others, demonstrating that by listening and doing all He could to help. When he died, I felt as if a part of my life was missing. Charles led many people to faith in Jesus Christ, but he always gave the glory to God. In all the years I served with him, I never heard him take any credit himself for the good things that were happening through his ministry.

A Place to Begin

Where do you stand on this issue? Does Jesus Christ get the glory in your life? Do your lips speak His praises, or do you tell what *you* have done and accomplished? Those who please God are those who give all the glory to Jesus Christ.

Chapter 3

The Glory of
the Cross

IF YOU WERE TO list the reasons the apostle Paul
was so effective as a first-century preacher, what
would you put on your list?

Attractive personality?
Well-liked by most people?
Brilliant intellectual?
Outstanding vocabulary and delivery?
Handsome in appearance?
Powerful speaking voice?

Those may well be standards we look for in our
preachers, but when Paul analyzed himself and the
reasons for his success he always focused on something quite different. "But may it never be that I
should boast, except in the cross of our Lord Jesus

Christ, through which the world has been crucified to me, and I to the world" (Gal. 6:14).

Paul never boasted about his abilities and talents. Rather, the message of the cross, he said, is something about which to boast. If we want to please God in our lives, then, like Paul, we should be proclaiming the message of the cross.

At one point in my ministry, I was experiencing a lack of joy and enthusiasm in preaching. I felt empty inside. I was losing motivation. During that dry period, I decided to read the life of Paul and try to discover the secrets of his success. Then I came across these words, which brought a new perspective to my heart: "For Christ did not send me to baptize, but to preach the gospel, not in cleverness of speech, that the cross of Christ should not be made void. For the word of the cross is to those who are perishing foolishness, but to us who are being saved it is the power of God" (1 Cor. 1:17,18). I continued to read, and discovered a wonderful truth in verse 21 of the same chapter: "For since in the wisdom of God the world through its wisdom did not come to know God, God was well-pleased through the foolishness of the message preached to save those who believe."

It is clear that God is "well-pleased" with the message of the cross. Yet under the sign of the cross much harm has been done. To many people the cross is a grim reminder of human brutality and the lengths to which religious people will go to persuade others.

The cross was made out of wood. There is no efficacy in that wood. Nothing magical should be as-

sociated with it. There is no need to kiss it or worship it. The gospel is not about a piece of wood—it
is about a Person who died on it: the Savior of the
world. When we refer to the message of the cross,
we are not talking about a religious symbol or an or-
nament to hang around one's neck. The gospel deals
with what Jesus Christ did when He died on that
cross.

Paul said, "For I determined to know nothing
among you except Jesus Christ, and Him crucified"
(1 Cor. 2:2). That is the message of the cross. When
we preach what Jesus did in dying for our sins on
the cross, God is pleased for two reasons: because
His power is displayed, and because His purpose is
established.

A. *God's power is displayed in the preaching of the
cross.*

For the word of the cross is to those who are perishing foolishness, but to us who are being saved *it is
the power of God.* For it is written, "I will destroy the
wisdom of the wise, And the cleverness of the clever
I will set aside." Where is the wise man? Where is
the scribe? Where is the debater of this age? Has not
God made foolish the wisdom of the world? For
since in the wisdom of God the world through its
wisdom did not come to know God, God was well-
pleased through the foolishness of the message
preached to save those who believe. For indeed Jews
ask for signs, and Greeks search for wisdom; but we
preach Christ crucified, to Jews a stumbling block,
and to Gentiles foolishness, but to those who are the
called, both Jews and Greeks, Christ the power of
God and the wisdom of God. Because the foolishness of God is wiser than men, and the weakness
of God is stronger than men (1 Cor. 1:18-25).

The message of the cross is the power of God because it works. It does what it claims. Its wisdom is found in the fact that it accomplishes its objective, the salvation of those who believe.

Verse 19, above, quotes from the book of Isaiah. The Old Testament context was when Sennacherib of Assyria was threatening Judah in the days of King Hezekiah. God promised deliverance. It would be His power that made the difference, not the manipulations of the politicians of Hezekiah's court. Their counsel, in fact, had led to the alliance with Egypt that had provoked the Assyrian invasion.

According to the Bible, the Lord rescued Judah from the hands of the Assyrian king through the intervention one night of the Angel of the Lord who killed 185,000 Assyrians in one blow. Judah was being challenged by God to trust Him completely and not depend on the wisdom and ways of the world.

In that sense, nothing much has changed today. The challenge to us is the same. We need to trust the message of the cross alone to do the work of God, not our human methods. We cannot persuade people by human reasoning to believe. We must put our confidence in the gospel itself. Can we say with Paul, "For I am not ashamed of the gospel, for *it is the power of God* for salvation to every one who believes, to the Jew first and also to the Greek. For in it the righteousness of God is revealed from faith to faith; as it is written, 'But the righteous man shall live by faith'" (Rom. 1:16,17).

The gospel *is* the power of God. We don't make it powerful by the way we speak. It does not become powerful if I am filled with the Holy Spirit—it already is powerful in and of itself. That's why God is pleased when the cross is preached and we trust it to accomplish His purpose, the salvation of those who believe.

It is a part of God's wisdom that the world through its own wisdom did not know Him (1 Cor. 1:21). God is honored through the plan He has designed. It doesn't glorify man, but rather God. It displays His grace from beginning to end.

The Jews of the first century were seeking for signs (1 Cor. 1:22) because the Old Testament promised that signs would make evident the identity of the Messiah. When Jesus came and made His messianic claims, the Jews wanted signs in the heavens, like those later predicted for the second coming of Christ. Yet signs of grace and mercy were clearly revealed in the miracles of Jesus Christ. Jesus said, "Believe Me that I am in the Father, and the Father in Me; otherwise believe on account of the works themselves" (Jn. 14:11).

Do you recall how He referred to His miracle of feeding the 5,000 with five barley loaves and two fish? "Truly, truly, I say to you [those present at the time], you seek Me, not because you saw signs, but because you ate of the loaves, and were filled. Do not work for the food which perishes, but for the food which endures to eternal life, which the Son of Man shall give to you, for on Him the Father, even God, has set His seal" (Jn. 6:26,27).

The people immediately responded, "What shall we do, that we may work the works of God?" (v. 28). "This is the work of God," Jesus replied, "that you believe in Him whom He has sent" (v. 29).

Years later in his Gospel the apostle John emphasized the importance of those signs. "Many other signs therefore Jesus also performed in the presence of the disciples, which are not written in this book; but these have been written that you may believe that Jesus is the Christ, the Son of God; and that believing you may have life in His name" (Jn. 20:30,31).

The Greeks of the first century were seeking wisdom. They wanted rational explanations of the universe. Their search was not for God, but for human wisdom. Such a search is futile, Paul said.

> For even though they knew God, they did not honor Him as God, or give thanks; but they became futile in their speculations, and their foolish heart was darkened. Professing to be wise, they became fools, and exchanged the glory of the incorruptible God for an image in the form of corruptible man and of birds and four-footed animals and crawling creatures (Rom. 1:21-23).

Some of those early hearers wanted the spectacular. Others wanted a logical explanation that fitted their own desires. As a result, the message of the cross became a stumbling block to the Jews, and seemed like foolishness to the Greeks (1 Cor. 1:23).

The cross called for an end to the ceremonial practices and sacrifices of the Old Testament. Jesus Christ was the final sacrifice for sins. So, to unbelieving Jews, the cross was a "death-trap" (that is what "stumbling block" means) to all that they held essential. The Greeks found the idea of the cross foolish. They couldn't see how the death and blood of one person could pay for the sins of others.

The secularist of our day says the same thing. The religionist of our day stumbles over the cross because it eliminates his religious system.

But how triumphantly Paul stated his conclusion: "The foolishness of God is wiser than men, and the weakness of God is stronger than men" (1 Cor. 1:25). The "foolishness of God" literally reads "the foolish thing [neuter] of God." That foolish thing in the context is the message of the cross. The "weakness of God" literally reads "the weak thing of God." That, too, refers to the cross. It may have seemed like weakness when Christ was captured by men and crucified, but it turned out to be the mighty power of God through which we are saved and our lives are changed.

Why is God pleased by the preaching of the cross? Because His power is displayed. The message of the cross, the gospel, is the power of God to all who believe.

B. *God's purpose is established by the preaching of the cross.*

The second reason why God is "well-pleased" by the preaching of the cross deals with His original purpose. He wants to be glorified. As has been said, the grand purpose of our lives is to glorify God. "Whether, then, you eat or drink or whatever you do, do all to the glory of God" (1 Cor. 10:31). Paul outlined this fact clearly in the remaining portion of 1 Corinthians 1, beginning with verse 26, and continuing on through chapter 2, verse 5:

> For consider your calling, brethren, that there were not many wise according to the flesh, not many mighty, not many noble; but God has chosen the

47

foolish things of the world to shame the wise, and God has chosen the weak things of the world to shame the things which are strong, and the base things of the world and the despised, God has chosen, the things that are not, that He might nullify the things that are, that no man should boast before God. But by His doing you are in Christ Jesus, who became to us wisdom from God, and righteousness and sanctification, and redemption, that just as it is written, "Let him who boasts, boast in the Lord." And when I came to you, brethren, I did not come with superiority of speech or of wisdom, proclaiming to you the testimony of God. For I determined to know nothing among you except Jesus Christ, and Him crucified. And I was with you in weakness and in fear and in much trembling. And my message and my preaching were not in persuasive words of wisdom, but in demonstration of the Spirit and of power, that your faith should not rest on the wisdom of men, but on the power of God.

The preaching of the cross eliminates boasting. Salvation is based on the plan and power of God, not on human ingenuity and cleverness.

In the above passage Paul listed seven things upon which our salvation is *not* based.

1. *Not on worldly importance.* Paul said, "not many wise . . . not many mighty, not many noble" (1 Cor. 1:26). He did not say "not *any*," but rather "not *many*." God's grace reaches to all, including society's upper classes.

2. *Not on our decision.* Three times Paul said, "God has chosen" (twice in v. 27 and once in v. 28). Some of us have the idea that God is fortunate to have us as one of His children. He ought to be thankful that we decided to accept His plan. We

think that we are wise for choosing Him. How foolish! God has chosen us, and that's why we are able to believe in Him. Jesus said, "You did not choose Me, but I chose you" (Jn. 15:16). Paul wrote, "just as He chose us in Him before the foundation of the world" (Eph. 1:4).

How important it is to understand that *He* chose *me*; I believed in Him because of His choice. We see a great illustration of God's choice in the case of Isaac's two sons, Jacob and Esau. "For though the twins were not yet born, and had not done anything good or bad, in order that God's purpose according to his choice might stand, not because of works, but because of Him who calls. . . ." (Rom. 9:11). This passage makes clear that God chose Jacob instead of Esau, even though Esau was the first-born son. God made the decision before the boys were born.

3. *Not on our personal worthiness.* Paul wrote that "God has chosen the foolish things of the world" (1 Cor. 1:27). His purpose in doing so was "to shame the wise." God did not say, "Because they have such great potential, I think I'll save them!" Ephesians 2:8 says "For by grace you have been saved through faith; and that not of yourselves, it is the gift of God." God's grace gives us what we don't deserve. Therefore there is hope for all of us, not just for those who show great potential.

4. *Not on our own ability.* Paul said that "God has chosen the weak things of the world" (1 Cor. 1:27). His purpose was "to shame the things which are strong." He does not save us because we have the ability to believe the message of the cross.

An elderly man once said to me, "I don't think

I have the strength to believe." I showed him from the Scriptures that salvation is based on God's power, not on our ability to believe. Our acceptance of Jesus Christ as our Savior from sin brings the miracle of spiritual birth. It is caused by God, not by us. Paul taught, "when I am weak, then I am strong" (2 Cor. 12:10). God displays His power in the "weak things of the world."

5. *Not on the family into which we were born.* When Paul wrote "the base things of the world" he was referring to the family into which we were born (1 Cor. 1:28). The word *base* in the sense of our birth is in contrast to the idea of being "well-born." God has chosen people whose family life is not the greatest. But that makes no difference to Him. We are not Christians because we were born of Christian parents. We are not excluded if our family is not very acceptable to most people. God chooses people who come from difficult backgrounds, even from what appears to be impossible family situations.

We can know for certain that the basis of His choice is not the family into which we were born. "But as many as received Him, to them He gave the right to become children of God, even to those who believe in His name, who were born not of blood, nor of the will of the flesh, nor of the will of man, but of God" (Jn. 1:12-13). Blood ties will not do. Our acceptability to God is the result of God's own choice.

6. *Not on what others think of us.* When Paul used the word "despised" in verse 28, a lot of people could identify with him. Pagan society often catalogued people, some as acceptable, some not. God enjoys picking the ones others would not. No

matter what other people think of you, God's plan is to save all those who believe. It is not based on the evaluations and opinions of others. For that, we can all be thankful.

7. *Not on anything that exists in us.* "God has chosen the things that are not, that He might nullify the things that are" (1 Cor. 1:28). Our possessions, the so-called "things" of life, don't bring happiness. Nor do they acquire for us the favor of God. We cannot earn what God offers us. Salvation (eternal life) is the gift of God (Rom. 6:23), "not as a result of works, that no one should boast" (Eph. 2:9).

How sad that so many people believe that the things they possess will somehow gain them all they need. Eternal life cannot be purchased by anything we have. Rather, it is given to all who believe that Jesus Christ died for their sins.

Paul frequently referred to his inadequacies and struggles, using words like "weakness" and "fear" and "much trembling" (1 Cor. 2:3-4). He did not speak in "persuasive words of wisdom," but instead about Jesus Christ and His death on the cross. Paul's words demonstrated the work of the Holy Spirit. The purpose of God was being established, "that your faith should not rest on the wisdom of men, but on the power of God" (1 Cor. 2:5).

Some of the mightiest influences in the history of the world have been the evangelists of the past 100 years. I love to read biographies like the amazing story of Dwight L. Moody, a shoe salesman who moved the hearts of millions toward the Lord. Moody's message was simple, direct, and centered in the cross of Jesus Christ. Billy Sunday was another such individual. And R. A. Torrey, though a master teacher, continued to preach and teach the glory of the cross. Bob Jones, Sr., John R. Rice, Billy Graham. All have been powerful preachers of their time. All have centered their message on the cross of Jesus Christ. And God is pleased with their proclamation.

The effect of the cross's message on believers was expressed by hymn writer Isaac Watts (1674-1748) in "When I Survey the Wondrous Cross":

When I survey the wondrous cross
On which the Prince of Glory died,
My richest gain I count but loss,
And pour contempt on all my pride.

Forbid it, Lord, that I should boast,
Save in the death of Christ, my God;
All the vain things that charm me most,
I sacrifice them to His blood.

See from His head, His hands, His feet,
Sorrow and love flow mingled down;
Did e'er such love and sorrow meet;
Or thorns compose so rich a crown?

Were the whole realm of nature mine,
That were a present far too small;
Love so amazing, so divine,
Demands my soul, my life, my all.

A Place to Begin

What things are you most proud of? How do you see God's hand in those matters? Do you admit that to others?

What has the gospel meant to you? Try to relate the seven factors listed in this chapter to your own experience of salvation.

52

Chapter 4

We Must Have Faith

AT TIMES FAITH appears to be "whistling in the dark"—or hoping that something is so when there is no evidence at all to prove it. The faith about which the Bible speaks is made of stronger stuff. It is based more on objective facts rather than on subjective feelings.

Hebrews 11:5 tells us that Enoch had faith, and because of it he was "pleasing God." God is pleased when we have faith. "And without faith it is impossible to please Him, for he who comes to God must believe that He is, and that He is a rewarder of those who seek Him" (Heb. 11:6).

A Definition of Faith

What kind of faith pleases God? Most of us recognize our need for some kind of faith; so many of our life experiences demonstrate that need. But a lot that is called *faith* is just "wishful thinking" or even "presumption." Many of us at times try to make ourselves believe something when we sincerely doubt its truthfulness. Consider what the Bible says about faith. "Now faith is the assurance of things hoped for, the conviction of things not seen. For by it the men of old gained approval. By faith we understand that the worlds were prepared by the word of God, so that what is seen was not made out of things which are visible" (Heb. 11:1-3).

In a class of high school students listening to a discussion about the origin of the solar system, one student disagreed with the teacher and the class. The viewpoint being presented was that of evolution. This student believed that the solar system was created by God. The teacher said to this student, "On what basis do you believe that God created the universe?" The student replied, "The same basis on which you believe in evolution." Surprised, the teacher asked, "What basis is that?" The student replied, "Faith. You have no more evidence that the universe simply happened than I have in believing that it was created by God. In fact, the evidence I see points to a Designer, not to chance or coincidence." The student was right. It is by faith that we perceive God's creation.

Rather than a definition, Hebrews 11:1-3 is a short explanation of faith, a description of what faith does. According to these verses, if faith is operating in your life, there will be two positive results: (*a*) assurance of future blessings, and (*b*) acceptance of present realities. The remaining verses of Hebrews

11 demonstrate these two results of faith in the lives of God's people. Some call this chapter the "Hall of Faith." The people listed were not super-saints. They had struggles just as we have. They experienced many barriers to faith as we also do. But their experiences are helpful in teaching us about the kind of faith that pleases God.

Faith Brings Assurance of Future Blessings

"Faith is the assurance of things hoped for." The word *assurance* means "to stand under." It was used in ancient times of a "title deed." So faith is the title deed of things for which we hope. Faith lends substance to the fact that what we hope for will really come to pass. This faith is based on the promises of God.

Faith Produces Acceptance of Present Realities

Faith is "the conviction of things not seen." The word *conviction* refers to proof, or the means of proof, that results in a person's being convinced. The things not being seen are described here by the use of a Greek word referring to what we practically experience now. (Our English word *pragmatic* comes from this Greek word.) What are we experiencing now that we cannot see, and which takes faith in order to be convinced of? The list could go on and on:

1. The existence of God
2. The presence of Christ at God's right hand
3. The intercession of Christ for us
4. Forgiveness of sins
5. Spiritual birth and growth

Faith in the promises of God gives us the conviction, or proof, that these things are real and not just imaginary. At lunch one day a businessman asked, "How do you know for sure that what you believe is true, really is?" Many people ask that question. The answer is faith. I believe the promises of God in the Bible. That means I believe that the Bible is totally reliable. I believe it is the Word of God to us. And that also takes faith.

It is impossible to please God without faith, yet at times it seems that we are asking people to accept something without evidence. Such is not the case. The record of the Scriptures alone gives us much reason for trusting God's promises in the future. What He has said and done in the past gives us ample proof to believe that His promises for the future will come to pass. The record of God's dealings with people in the past is the point behind Hebrews 11. The combined testimony of these people of faith, these witnesses to what God did, should cause us to put our trust in Him. That's why Hebrews 12:1-2 reads the way it does:

> Therefore, since we have so great a cloud of witnesses [Hebrews 11] surrounding us, let us also lay aside every encumbrance, and the sin which so easily entangles us, and let us run with endurance the race that is set before us, fixing our eyes on Jesus, the author and perfecter of faith, who for the joy set before Him endured the cross, despising the shame, and has sat down at the right hand of the throne of God.

The Cloud of Witnesses

Eleven people are discussed in some detail in Hebrews 11:4-31. Six more names are mentioned in verse 32 along with other references to "the prophets" who suffered greatly (vv. 33-38). A summary of these witnesses is then given: "And all these, having gained approval through their faith, did not receive what was promised, because God had provided something better for us, so that apart from us they should not be made perfect" (Heb. 11:39-40).

They believed God (and therefore were pleasing to God) even though they did not receive what was promised to them. They, along with all of us who also will believe God's promises, will one day be rewarded for having faith and confidence in God's Word.

Jesus said to Thomas who demanded evidence that Jesus really arose from the dead, "Because you have seen Me, have you believed? Blessed are they who did not see, and yet believed" (Jn. 20:29).

In the story of the rich man and Lazarus in Luke 16, the rich man claimed that some evidence of what life is like in hell would persuade his five brothers. He asked Abraham to send someone to warn them. Abraham replied, "They have Moses and the Prophets; let them hear them" (Lk. 16:29). The rich man answered: "No, Father Abraham, but if someone goes to them from the dead, they will repent!" (v. 30). How did Abraham reply? "If they do not listen to Moses and the Prophets, neither will they be persuaded if someone rises from the dead" (v. 31).

That is still true today. Many people want more proof than the promises of God's Word. Yet God is pleased when we put our faith in what He has said, regardless of whether we ever see those promises fulfilled in our lifetimes.

Let's now consider how each of those eleven witnesses demonstrated a faith that was pleasing to God.

1. *Abel* (Heb. 11:4). Abel's faith was pleasing to God because he brought the sacrifice that God wanted, rather than the product of his own hands like his brother Cain. "For this is the message which you have heard from the beginning, that we should love one another; not as Cain, who was of the evil one, and slew his brother. And for what reason did he slay him? Because his deeds were evil, and his brother's were righteous" (1 Jn. 3:11-12).

Faith understands that God's ways are not our ways. So many people try to come to God on their own terms. What pleases God is our faith in His plan, along with our refusal to trust our own works as providing evidence of our righteousness.

2. *Enoch* (Heb. 11:5). Enoch's faith was pleasing to God because he "walked with God," and believed that what God had predicted about the future would come true. Enoch prophesied God's message when he said: "Behold, the Lord came with many thousands of His holy ones, to execute judgment upon all, and to convict all the ungodly of all their ungodly deeds which they have done in an ungodly way, and of all the harsh things which ungodly sinners have spoken against Him" (Jude 14-15).

The judgment which God predicted would come upon an ungodly generation came at the time of Noah through a flood. The faith of Enoch was so strong, that he named his son *Methusaleh*, which means "when he dies, it shall come or be done." The exact year of his death was the year in which the flood came. Enoch pleased God because he trusted God's Word. His continual walk with God was evidence that he was a true believer. There are many promises in the Bible about God bringing judgment upon this world. Do you believe that it will happen?

3. *Noah* (Heb. 11:7). God told Noah to build an ark because He was going to destroy the world with a flood. Now Noah had never seen a flood. He had never seen an ark, but he went ahead and did what God told him to do. His faith, therefore, was pleasing to God. Obedience to what God says is evidence of the validity of the faith we say we have in Him and His Word.

4. *Abraham* (Heb. 11:8-10). A great deal is said about the faith of Abraham, the father of us all. Abraham's faith was pleasing to God because he believed that God's promise to him would be fulfilled even when it meant leaving his own country and relatives. He believed God's promise about having children like the sand of the seashore and the stars of the sky even when he was too old to have a son, and his wife, too, was aged and barren. He believed God's promise to him even when God later asked him to offer up that son, Isaac, as a sacrifice. Abraham was fully confident that God would raise Isaac from the dead (cf. Heb. 11:17-19)

Abraham's hope did not rest in the real estate of this earth. He looked for a better country, a "heavenly one" (v. 16). Because of his faith and that of others like him, God "has prepared a city for them." Heaven will reward all who have trusted God and His Word.

5. *Sarah* (Heb. 11:11-12). Credit must also go to Sarah, who had to struggle with what God promised in spite of her age and her inability to have children. She "considered Him faithful who had promised." That's the key to the kind of faith that pleases God. Our faith must be in the existence and character of God Himself. When we realize who God is, it will be easier for us to believe in what He says.

6. *Isaac* (Heb. 11:20). It took great faith and trust on Isaac's part to allow his father to tie him up like an animal sacrifice and draw the knife. Many years later, Isaac's faith was still pleasing God. He trusted God to fulfill His word about his sons even though when he was old and blind he had made a mistake about which one was to be blessed.

7. *Jacob* (Heb. 11:21). Jacob's faith was pleasing to God because he blessed the sons of Joseph (Ephraim and Manasseh) as God told him to do, rather than go along with the customary first-born right.

8. *Joseph* (Heb. 11:22). Joseph's faith was pleasing to God when he requested his bones to be taken up from Egypt to the promised land. He believed that God would someday take His people out of Egypt. God had promised that to his great grandfather Abraham, and Joseph believed God's promise.

9. *Moses* (Heb. 11:23-29). Much attention is given to the great Hebrew leader, Moses. Moses' faith was pleasing to God when he refused to be called the son of Pharaoh's daughter. He had the opportunity for high position and great political power, but he chose to suffer with God's people and to bear "the reproaches of Christ" instead of all the

treasures and prestige which Egypt of that day could offer him. His faith was pleasing to God when he did not fear the wrath of the king because his confidence was in God whom he could not see. His faith was honored when he kept the Passover in obedience to what God told him to do. His faith pleased God when he dared to lead the children of Israel across the dry land of the split Red Sea, as the water on both sides was being held back by a strong east wind provided by God.

Moses is a reminder of the constant temptations this world offers. Many of us are willing to forget God's promises for a moment of wealth or pleasure. Faith that pleases God is willing to suffer if necessary, knowing that ultimately we will be rewarded.

10. *Joshua* (Heb. 11:30). Though unmentioned by name, it is clear that this verse refers to Joshua, who led the children of Israel into the land of Canaan. The first problem was the fortress of Jericho—yet faith in God won the day. The Israelites marched around the city once each day for six days, and seven times on the seventh day. As they completed that thirteenth trip, the walls came tumbling down. "By faith the walls of Jericho fell down." The children of Israel, no doubt, felt quite foolish in marching like that around the city. But God had promised victory. The story is a memorial to the kind of faith that pleases God.

11. *Rahab* (Heb. 11:31). Rahab's faith was pleasing to God when she welcomed the spies, accepting the fact that God had given the children of Israel the land in which she lived. She believed in the God of Israel and His power. Her faith was the kind that works (Jms. 2:17-26). God honored her by allowing

her marriage to Salmon, a man in the messianic line. She had a famous son named Boaz, the grandfather of King David.

Gideon, Barak, Samson, and Jephthah all lived in the period of the judges (Heb. 11:32). Their victories were based on their confidence in God's word, not in their own ability and military might. The names of David, Samuel, and the prophets likewise bring to our attention people who had to trust God in difficult circumstances. The sufferings of God's servants as described in Hebrews 11:33-38, as well as the victories, are reminders of what it means to trust God.

God is pleased when we believe Him, especially when times are tough and our struggles cause us to question what He has promised. How important to remember apostle Paul's words: "For I consider that the sufferings of this present time are not worthy to be compared with the glory that is to be revealed to us" (Rom. 8:18).

Again, we have this encouraging word:

Therefore we do not lose heart, but though our outer man is decaying, yet our inner man is being renewed day by day. For momentary, light affliction is producing for us an eternal weight of glory far beyond all comparison, while we look not at the things which are seen, but at the things which are not seen; for the things which are seen are temporal, but the things which are not seen are eternal (2 Cor. 4:16-18).

That's the secret. We have to keep our eyes on what is coming, on the things that God has promised. We have to believe His Word, not our circumstances. That kind of faith truly pleases God.

When we question His Word, we obviously are not pleasing Him and are therefore not fulfilling the ultimate purpose He has for us.

Those past heroes of faith are inspiring, but when we learn of a contemporary who has demonstrated great faith in the midst of suffering, it often has deeper impact upon us. When I first saw the film *The Hiding Place*, the marvelous story of Corrie ten Boom, I cried frequently during the movie. Tears do not come easily for me, but the faith of that Christian woman in the midst of such difficult times spoke to my heart. I kept asking, "Would I be able to have faith under such terrible circumstances?" It seemed to me in viewing that film that the only way any of us can endure such suffering, and maintain great hope in the Lord and the future, is by keeping our eyes on Him. It is the assurance of His presence, power, protection, and promises that keeps hope alive in our hearts.

A Place to Begin

If someone asked you what your faith means to you, how would you explain it? Does your faith have elements of presumption or wishful thinking?

What assurance about the future has your faith brought you? What present realities is it helping you to accept? Write these ideas down (with today's date) and keep it for future reference.

I love these words written in 1787 by George Keith:

How firm a foundation, ye saints of the Lord,
Is laid for your faith in His excellent Word!
What more can He say than to you He hath said
To you, who for refuge to Jesus have fled?

Fear not, I am with thee - O be not dismayed,
For I am thy God, I will still give thee aid;
I'll strengthen thee, help thee, and cause thee to stand,
Upheld by my gracious omnipotent hand.

When thru' the deep waters I call thee to go,
The rivers of woe shall not thee overflow;
For I will be with thee thy troubles to bless,
And sanctify to thee thy deepest distress.

When thru' fiery trials thy pathway shall lie,
My grace, all-sufficient, shall be thy supply;
The flame shall not hurt thee - I only design
Thy dross to consume and thy gold to refine.

The soul that on Jesus hath leaned for repose,
I will not, I will not desert to his foes;
That soul, tho all hell should endeavor to shake,
I'll never - no, never - no, never forsake!

Chapter 5

Why Wisdom Pleases God

HAVE YOU EVER been faced with a decision involving two possibilities or opportunities and had absolutely no idea which one to choose? When I face that problem, as I frequently do, it reminds me how much I need the wisdom of God.

My need of wisdom came to me forcefully when I was trying to decide which college I should attend and why. There were several possibilities. Again with graduate school there were a number of possibilities, and again they all looked good. When I started thinking seriously about marriage, I found that I liked several young women, and again I wondered how I was ever going to make the right decision. (When I met my wife, *that* decision was simple—there was no one as wonderful as she is—and

65

after raising three children and being her companion all these years, I still feel the same.)

Decisions. Why are there so many of them? How do you know what to do every time? The more knowledge you have doesn't seem to make the process any easier. So our need of wisdom is constant, through all of life.

God says a lot about wisdom in His Word and why we need it. How tragic that so many of us fail to heed that advice. The counsel of the ungodly is often what we believe and accept, rather than what God says.

Proverbs is a "wisdom book," written in large part by Solomon, the wisest of ancient kings. He urged us to seek wisdom. "Make your ear attentive to wisdom, Incline your heart to understanding; For if you cry for discernment, Lift your voice for understanding; If you seek her as silver, And search for her as for hidden treasures; Then you will discern the fear of the LORD, And discover the knowledge of God" (Prov. 2:2-5).

Solomon knew about wisdom firsthand. "How blessed is the man who finds wisdom, And the man who gains understanding. For its profit is better than the profit of silver, And its gain than fine gold. She is more precious than jewels; And nothing you desire compares with her. Long life is in her right hand; In her left hand are riches and honor. Her ways are pleasant ways, And all her paths are peace. She is a tree of life to those who take hold of her, And happy are all who hold her fast" (Prov. 3:13-18).

God gave Solomon the opportunity to ask for

anything his heart desired. Solomon's response to God's invitation is worthy of serious reflection. It shows us how we can please God. Let's look at that story in 1 Kings 3. Solomon said to God:

> Thou hast shown great lovingkindness to Thy servant David my father, according as he walked before Thee in truth and righteousness and uprightness of heart toward Thee; and Thou hast reserved for him this great lovingkindness, that Thou hast given him a son to sit on his throne, as it is this day. And now, O LORD my God, Thou hast made Thy servant king in place of my father David; yet I am but a little child: I do not know how to go out or come in. And Thy servant is in the midst of Thy people which Thou hast chosen, a great people who cannot be numbered or counted for multitude. So give Thy servant an understanding heart to judge Thy people to discern between good and evil. For who is able to judge this great people of Thine? (vv. 6-9).

Solomon knew his inadequacies and the way in which God had dealt with his father David. He acknowledged the lovingkindness of God, and the fact that he truly saw himself as God's servant. His attitude was right. "And it was pleasing in the sight of the Lord that Solomon had asked this thing" (1 Kgs. 3:10).

Asking for wisdom pleases God. Trusting our own intelligence and evaluations does not. God said,

> Because you have asked this thing and have not asked for yourself long life, nor have asked riches for yourself, nor have you asked for the life of your enemies, but have asked for yourself discernment to understand justice, behold, I have done according to your words. Behold, I have given you a wise and

discerning heart, so that there has been no one like you before you, nor shall one like you arise after you. And I have also given you what you have not asked, both riches and honor, so that there will not be any among the kings like you all your days. And if you walk in My ways, keeping My statutes and commandments, as your father David walked, then I will prolong your days (1 Kgs. 3:11-14).

What a tremendous opportunity Solomon received from God. God honors everyone who wants wisdom. Further, He was so pleased that Solomon asked for wisdom, he gave him riches and honor as well.

Acquire wisdom! Acquire understanding! Do not forget, nor turn away from the words of my mouth. Do not forsake her, and she will guard you; Love her, and she will watch over you. The beginning of wisdom is: Acquire wisdom; And with all your acquiring, get understanding. Prize her, and she will exalt you; She will honor you if you embrace her. She will place on your head a garland of grace; She will present you with a crown of beauty (Prov. 4:5-9).

Wisdom comes from knowing God and His ways and words. "The fear of the LORD is the beginning of wisdom, And the knowledge of the Holy One is understanding" (Prov. 9:10). We need to know God in order to be wise. When we want what we want, we are beginning to understand what it means to please Him.

Wisdom, therefore, is crucial to learning how to please God. It is the opposite of trusting yourself. It is contrary to all attempts of the self to achieve and to perform.

How Do We Get Wisdom?

Studying the Bible brings knowledge and also teaches us the qualities and actions of wisdom. The term *wisdom* implies both knowledge and understanding, but suggests skill in using them both. Wisdom is the application of knowledge. Wisdom is available to all believers. How do we get it?

> But if any of you lacks wisdom, let him ask of God, who gives to all men generously and without reproach, and it will be given to him. But let him ask in faith without any doubting, for the one who doubts is like the surf of the sea driven and tossed by the wind. For let not that man expect that he will receive anything from the Lord, being a double-minded man, unstable in all his ways (Jms. 1:5-8).

That passage outlines four specific steps about how to get wisdom.

1. *We must recognize our need for God's wisdom.* Solomon knew his need for wisdom. Do we? James 1:5 begins, "If any of you lacks wisdom." The word *if* means "if and it is so." We might translate in English, "Since you lack wisdom." A major difficulty in our present culture is our failure to see our need. We are so occupied with attempts to convince ourselves how capable we are that we fail to see our need. It seems that the mottos of our day are "Believe in yourself," "You can do it if you want to," "You have great potential," etc. There are elements of truth in all of those slogans (and in many more like them), but there is also one serious deficiency. The more we see the answers in ourselves, the less we will see our need of God's help.

God is pleased when we sense our need of wisdom. The truth is, we all lack His wisdom. It is not found within; it comes from above.

The secular humanism of our day has eliminated many people's sense of their need for God and His help. Why should we call on God? What can He do about our worries and struggles? A lot of people believe that if there is a God, He is not concerned with people's individual problems. That's what a young salesman told me. He was struggling with some personal difficulties, and when I suggested he look to the Lord for answers, he said he didn't need a crutch. He felt that in time he could work things out. It's been over a year now, and he still hasn't solved anything. He's looking within himself for the answers, and that's not where they are found.

God is pleased when we cry out for His help. "For we do not have a high priest who cannot sympathize with our weaknesses, but one who has been tempted in all things as we are, yet without sin. Let us therefore draw near with confidence to the throne of grace, that we may receive mercy and may find grace to help in time of need" (Heb. 4:15-16). God invites us to come to Him and find the resources we need.

2. *We must realize how God gives His wisdom.* James 1:5 says, "Let him ask of God." God is the One who will give us the wisdom we need. What pleases Him is when we come to Him, believing in Him and in what He can do (Heb. 11:6). It sounds so simple to ask, but until we do, we will never receive. We frequently ask others for advice. Why are we so slow to turn to the God who made us and knows all our needs?

"For the Lord God is a sun and shield; the Lord gives grace and glory; No good thing does He withhold from those who walk uprightly" (Ps. 84:11). We have a loving Father who desires to give good things to His children.

> For everyone who asks, receives; and he who seeks, finds; and to him who knocks, it shall be opened. Now suppose one of you fathers is asked by his son for a fish; he will not give him a snake instead of a fish, will he? Or if he is asked for an egg, he will not give him a scorpion, will he? If you then, being evil, know how to give good gifts to your children, how much more shall your heavenly Father give the Holy Spirit to those who ask Him? (Lk. 11:10-13).

The way God gives is an encouragement to seek His wisdom. James 1:5 describes at least three ways in which God gives His wisdom to those who ask Him for it.

(*a*) God gives His wisdom continually. James says, "who gives to all men." The word *gives* is in the present tense, indicating a continuing process. God keeps on giving; He doesn't stop. The English translation "men" here is of course generic. It means He gives wisdom to all who ask: men, women, even children.

(*b*) God gives His wisdom generously. The text reads, "who gives to all men generously." The root of that adverb means "to stretch or spread out." It reminds us that God's resources and generosity are unlimited. His supply of wisdom never runs out.

(*c*) God gives His wisdom tenderly. James also says that God gives to all persons "without reproach." That means He doesn't rebuke us for our lack of wisdom. He does not condemn us for it. That is a wonderful characteristic of our God. "Just as a father has compassion on his children, So the LORD has compassion on those who fear Him. For He Himself knows our frame; He is mindful that we are but dust" (Ps. 103:13-14).

3. *We must rely on God's promise to give wisdom.* Here our faith comes into the picture. James says at the end of verse 5, "and it will be given to him." That's a promise from God. Too often we doubt at this point. We wonder if God means what He says—which leads us to our final point.

4. *We must respond in faith, not doubt.* James 1:6 says, "But let him ask in faith without any doubting." To doubt is like praying for rain, but not taking your umbrella. The root word behind *doubting* implies your separating the possible from the impossible. It means you do your own evaluation of something and come to the conclusion that God cannot do anything about it.

A person who doubts is "like the surf of the sea driven and tossed by the wind." Perhaps you have experienced that kind of emotional turmoil. I recognize the illustration quite well! When I question what God can do, it shows in the way I handle a given situation. I lack determination and conviction.

What are the consequences of doubting? "For let not that man expect that he will receive anything from the Lord, being a double-minded man, unstable in all his ways" (Jms. 1:7-8).

There I see two consequences of doubting God: (1) inability to understand or react properly to trials and difficulties (lack of wisdom, v. 7); (2) instability in handling our trials and difficulties (v. 8). The "double-minded" person of verse eight is referring literally to someone who has "two souls." He or she is going off in two different directions.

The Results of Having God's Wisdom

The apostle Paul discusses the results of having God's wisdom like this:

> For this reason also, since the day we heard of it, we have not ceased to pray for you and to ask that you may be filled with the knowledge of His will in all spiritual wisdom and understanding, so that you may walk in a manner worthy of the Lord, *to please Him in all respects*, bearing fruit in every good work and increasing in the knowledge of God; strengthened with all power, according to His glorious might, for attaining of all steadfastness and patience; joyously giving thanks to the Father, who has qualified us to share in the inheritance of the saints in light. For He delivered us from the domain of darkness, and transferred us to the kingdom of His beloved Son, in whom we have redemption, the forgiveness of sins (Col. 1:9-14).

God's ultimate objective for all believers is that we live lives that are pleasing to Him, bringing Him glory and praise. The key to pleasing God "in all respects" (v. 10) is to be "filled with the knowledge of His will in all spiritual wisdom and understanding." We desperately need God's perspective; our failure to have it keeps us from pleasing Him.

The wonderful results of being a man or woman who has God's wisdom and understanding, who truly pleases God in every way, are pictured in four participles in these verses that describe a wise, godly lifestyle.

1. *Our actions*—"bearing fruit in every good work." Another way of putting this would be, "being controlled by the Holy Spirit in everything we do." We know that the Holy Spirit produces the fruit (Gal. 5:22-23). When we have God's wisdom, we will be bearing His fruit. Our actions (and reactions) reveal whether or not we have God's wisdom.

2. *Our aim in life*—"increasing in the knowledge of God." The goal of a man or woman who is filled with God's wisdom is to know God better each day. A mark of maturity in the Christian life is when all our pursuits are submitted to this one great priority: knowing God. When God's wisdom is filling our life, our knowledge of God continues to increase.

3. *Our ability to handle things*—"strengthened with all power, according to His glorious might, for the attaining of all steadfastness and patience." No problem or burden or crisis that we face will be greater than the power of God within us to meet it. Ability to endure tough times and difficult situations comes from God. When we are filled with His wisdom, our lives are strengthened with spiritual power. Pleased with our quest for wisdom, God rewards us with strength to handle life's trials.

4. *Our attitude toward all things*—"joyously giving thanks to the Father." God's wisdom helps us to be thankful for everything that happens. First, we understand it better. Second, God puts His peace into our heart. We stop trying to solve things ourselves, and we begin to rely more and more on Him. We know that He can work in everything for good. "In everything give thanks; for this is God's will for you in Christ Jesus" (1 Thess. 5:18).

I was returning from a week of preaching at a Christian camp, enjoying a beautiful night and a lovely six-hour drive home, when I had a flat tire. Without a moment's hesitation I jumped out of the car, singing as I went to the trunk of the car, removed the jack, and began to change the tire. I thought to myself at the time that I was really coping with this annoyance with grace. I was pretty well convinced that I must be Spirit-filled that evening to be handling it with such joy. Back in my car, continuing to sing, I went about ten more miles and had another flat. By then I was fifty miles from any gas station and it was three A.M. Boy, was I mad! I said, "Thanks a lot, God. Is this what I get for all I've done for you?"

To make a long story short (including the circumstances of my getting home), I learned a big lesson that night. Giving thanks was easy for one flat tire, but not for two. It brought home to me how much I need the wisdom and understanding of God.

A Place to Begin

A great way to start learning about God's wisdom and how to apply it is to read the book of Proverbs. There are thirty-one chapters, one for each day of the month. Proverbs can be studied in many different ways, but one way that helps me is to do it by subjects. I take a piece of paper and put a subject at the top that I want to study. For instance, the word *finances*. Then I write down each principle or insight from the book of Proverbs that deals with that subject. After putting them all down, I then organize the material into sub-topics, like "debt" or "loaning money" or "saving" or "spending," etc. I have discovered that the principles I learn are needed in my life continually. After identifying a particular principle, I then pray and ask God to help me apply it.

Chapter 6

The Problem of Sensuality

THE "AGE OF THE SELF" is synonymous with sensuality. Selfism and sensuality go together. When the focus is on ourselves and our needs, we soon get around to the physical and begin to "see things differently." Having sex with someone may then be described as "ministering to a person's need," language that used to refer to spiritual gifts as we Christians would use that phrase.

A man sitting in my office was trying to explain the *whys* of his adulterous affair. He said, "I had tremendous needs at the moment, and she was able to meet them. I know you think it's wrong, but if it wasn't God's will, then I wouldn't have such tremendous needs for it." As a Christian who had gotten caught up in the philosophy of selfism, he was now bringing God into the picture, attempting to justify what he had done.

He went on: "Everything isn't black and white, as you often say. People have needs and those needs must be met!" Now *he* was preaching. After listening to about thirty minutes of that, I decided it was time to change the focus. "Do you believe in God?" I asked. "Of course," he said. "Does what He has to say mean anything to you?" Getting irritated, he replied, "Sure it does." "Do you understand from the Bible that you will one day stand before God to give an account of what you have done, said, and thought?" "I think so," he said. "Do you believe that God has a right to judge us and chasten us when we do wrong?" I asked.

At that point he said, "I don't like the way this conversation is going. You're trying to make me feel guilty for what I've done!" "No," I said, "You are already guilty because of what God has said. The question now is, are you willing to admit that what you have done is wrong, confess it to God, and repent of it?" From that point on, things began to change in his heart. He did repent of his sin that day and is now back with his wife, rejoicing in God's plan for sex and marriage.

It doesn't always happen that way, however. Many people are unwilling to face the facts of God's Word. Their problem is self. If our goal in life is to please ourselves, then at some point our sexual desires will be affected. Before long we run into the *Playboy* philosophy of Hugh Hefner. That's where hedonism usually leads—to sexual freedom and indulgence. "If you feel a need for sex, then you have a right to have it": so the logic goes. Moral codes take effect only if your motivations are wrong.

The mid-sixties brought the rise of what was termed "a new morality," along with its underlying philosophy, "situation ethics." It's okay (according to that view) to have sex with someone other than your marital partner as long as you both are willing and don't intend to hurt anyone by your actions. That kind of rationale dominates what I call the cult of the self. No consideration is given to what God has said in His Word. The important thing is to take care of yourself, to see that your own needs are fulfilled.

Sexual immorality is always condemned by God in no uncertain terms. That means all sexual acts outside of marriage. God says you are not pleasing Him when such behavior is part of your life. Let us consider carefully what the apostle Paul wrote about this matter.

> Finally then, brethren, we request and exhort you in the Lord Jesus, that, as you received from us *instruction as to how you ought to walk and please God* (just as you actually do walk), that you may excel still more. For you know what commandments we gave you by the authority of the Lord Jesus. For this is the will of God, your sanctification; that is, that you *abstain from sexual immorality*; that each of you know how to possess his own vessel in sanctification and honor, not in lustful passion, like the Gentiles who do not know God; and that no man transgress and defraud his brother in the matter because the Lord is the avenger in all these things, just as we also told you before and solemnly warned you. For God has not called us for the purpose of impurity, but in sanctification. Consequently, he who rejects this is not rejecting man but the God who gives

His Holy Spirit to you (1 Thess. 4:1-8).

In order to please God, we are commanded to abstain from sexual immorality. That's clear. The doctrine of self-love teaches otherwise. It views God's instructions as restrictive and harsh, lacking in love and understanding of human need. But God, if He is God, knows our needs better than we do. He created our bodies fully understanding sexual desire and how it is to be fulfilled.

"But do not let immorality or any impurity or greed even be named among you, as is proper among saints; and there must be no filthiness and silly talk, or coarse jesting, which are not fitting, but rather giving of thanks" (Eph. 5:3-4). Verse 10 adds: "trying to learn what is pleasing to the Lord." Sexual immorality is obviously not pleasing to Him. We please God when we stay away from sexual sin.

The problem of sensuality centers in the human heart. The Bible speaks of "lust" in the sense of its being the desire to have sex contrary to God's commands. Jesus said, "For out of the heart come evil thoughts, murders, adulteries, fornications, thefts, false witness, slanders" (Mt. 15:19). The parallel passage in Mark 7:20-23 expands that statement like this: "That which proceeds out of the man, that is what defiles the man. For from within, out of the heart of men, proceed the evil thoughts and fornications, thefts, murders, adulteries, deeds of coveting and wickedness, as well as deceit, sensuality, envy, slander, pride and foolishness. All these evil things proceed from within and defile the man."

So the problem arises from our hearts, not from our cultural environment—which brings a certain clarity to the issue of pleasing God. It's a matter of the heart. We will not be able to please God in our actions if we lose the battle with lust in the heart. Jesus put it this way. "You have heard that it was said, 'You shall not commit adultery'; but I say to you, that everyone who looks on a woman to lust for her has committed adultery with her already in his heart" (Mt. 5:27-28). That is strong language, but He pinpoints where the problem lies. Lust is not love, but love is often used as an excuse for lust.

The apostle James described the process of lust with powerful imagery. "Let no one say when he is tempted, "I am being tempted by God'; for God cannot be tempted by evil, and He Himself does not tempt anyone. But each one is tempted when he is carried away and enticed by his own lust. Then when lust has conceived, it gives birth to sin; and when sin is accomplished, it brings forth death" (James 1:13-15).

This passage assumes that we all have "lust." When we are tempted to sin, however, God does not do the tempting. He never entices anyone to commit sin. He wants us to avoid sin. The temptation to commit sin is caused by the lust of our own hearts. We have no one to blame except ourselves. Beautiful women have traditionally been regarded as a "temptation," and the early Jewish commentators and church fathers sometimes went to shocking lengths in venting their misogyny. Yet women *per se* are not to be blamed for being physically attractive to men, nor are they the real problem. The problem is created within us. That's where we get "carried away and enticed."

Here we have the illustration of the conception

and birth of a baby. When "lust" (or sexual desire) conceives, it gives birth to sin. We might conclude, therefore, that the lust is not sinful in itself. God created us with sexual desires. The lust becomes a matter of sin, whether in mind or body, when we allow it to violate God's Word. When that sexual desire is directed toward one's spouse, there is no sin. When we seek sexual satisfaction with someone other than our marital partner, it becomes sin.

Many Christian men are troubled over this biblical teaching. Sexual desire occurs so frequently in their thought life that it appears to be almost a losing battle. How does one keep from sinning? If we please God by avoiding sexual sin, what hope do we have of ever pleasing Him? Good questions.

In attempting to answer those questions about the problem of sensuality, we need to look at some facts.

1. Sexual desire is not sinful.

2. Sexual immorality (the wrong use of sexual desire) is always sinful.

3. God never tempts any of us to commit sexual sin.

4. When we commit sin, we do so because we want to carry out our sexual desire. We have no one else to blame—not the circumstances, not our environment.

5. Sex within marriage is never condemned or minimized.

6. Sexual immorality is an act that deliberately resists the Holy Spirit and violates the law of God. Further, it affects our physical body.

To know those facts and believe them is one thing. To live them out is another matter. How do we do it? "But I say, walk by the Spirit," the apostle Paul wrote, "and you will not carry out the desire of the flesh. For the flesh sets its desire against the Spirit, and the Spirit against the flesh; for these are in opposition to one another, so that you may not do the things that you please" (Gal. 5:16-17). He does not say that we will get rid of the fleshly desires if we "walk by the Spirit." He said we wouldn't carry them out or fulfill them.

Paul wrote, "Flee immorality. Every other sin that a man commits is outside the body, but the immoral man sins against his own body" (1 Cor. 6:18). His point, I believe, refers to more than sexual disease, though that is often the result of continous immorality. The sexual vitality of a person's life can be diminished greatly through sexual immorality. The emotional and psychological factors related to proper sexual activity are greatly affected by immorality.

God's laws are not intended to keep us from having fun. They are all designed for our good. They will promote our happiness over the long haul. God, who knows the processes of the physical body better than any of us does, has given His sexual laws to protect us from harm and to insure a long and happy life that continues to bring sexual satisfaction.

How Can we Please God in the Use of our Sexual Desires?

Our heavenly Father is pleased, as most parents are, when their children are obedient. "And whatever we ask we receive from Him, because we keep

His commandments and do the things that are pleasing in His sight" (1 Jn. 3:22). We please God when we determine not to carry out our lustful impulses or desires. We please God when we decide to find fulfillment only with the person to whom we are married. "Now concerning the things about which you wrote, it is good for a man not to touch a woman. But because of immoralities, let each man have his own wife, and let each woman have her own husband" (1 Cor. 7:1-2).

God is pleased when we do what He says. His will for those with strong sexual desire is that they find fulfillment within the bonds of matrimony. Only that makes sense. The keys to satisfying sex lie in the areas of intimate friendship, loyalty, marital fidelity. It is mutual trust and strong commitment that insure a satisfying sexual relationship.

I was talking with a young man in his twenties, not married, who was having problems controlling himself sexually. He confessed, "My desires are so strong, I can't help having sex. I wish I could control them, but I can't." When I told him he should be thankful to God for giving him such strong desire, he seemed surprised and a little shocked. I encouraged him to consider marriage as God's will for his life, based on the strong sexual desires that God had given him. "What do I do in the meantime," he said, "until I find the right person to marry?" I said, "You will need the help of the Holy Spirit of God. You must make the decision in your heart to stay away from sexual sin." He repeated, "But my desires are so strong, I can't control them!"

I encouraged him that the Bible teaches that you *can* control them. That young man, in reality, was blaming God for giving him such strong desires; he was using that as an excuse for his lack of self-control (see 2 Tim. 1:7). A lot of us reason like that, especially when lust is controlling the way we think, instead of God's love and power through the Holy Spirit.

As our conversation continued, I discovered that this young man spent a good deal of time reading pornographic literature. No wonder he was having a problem controlling himself sexually. When he made a commitment to get that junk out of his life, the sexual pressure became tolerable and controllable. These decisions are made in the heart. That's where the battle must be won.

The Results of Sensuality

We face serious problems when we decide to engage in sexual immorality, yet those consequences are often ignored by the person choosing that route. When pleasing yourself, meeting your own needs, becomes a great obsession, sexual impurity often results. What are its consequences? Let me discuss three of them here.

1. *Lack of sexual vitality and possibility of sexual disease.* Back in the Old Testament "wisdom literature," we have this interesting passage:

Now then, my sons, listen to me,
And do not depart from the words of my mouth.
Keep your way far from her,
And do not go near the door of her house,
Lest you give your vigor to others,
And your years to the cruel one;
Lest strangers be filled with your strength,
And your hard-earned goods go to the house of an

alien;
And you groan at your latter end,
When your flesh and your body are consumed;
And you say, "How I have hated instruction!
And my heart spurned reproof!
And I have not listened to the voice of my teachers,
Nor inclined my ear to my instructors!
I was almost in utter ruin
In the midst of the assembly and congregation
(Prov. 5:7-14).

The terms *vigor* and *strength* are probable references to sexual vitality. The possibility of sexual disease is implied in the phrase, "when your flesh and your body are consumed." Pleasing God by obeying His sexual laws leads to our good and blessing. The consequences of sexual immorality are not often seen immediately, but become evident in time. As we grow older, we reap what we have sown. The damage has been done. God's grace and forgiveness are wonderful, and—praise the Lord—we can get a new start if we do wrong. But the scars of our actions and attitudes often remain, and they are a terrible price to pay.

2. *Lack of fellowship with God's people.* In the church of Corinth it seems that one member was guilty of incest, but that person and the sin were being tolerated rather than condemned. Paul wrote instructions to those believers about how to deal with that serious situation. According to this passage, Christians are not to associate with any so-called Christians who continue in particular sins, including immorality.

I wrote you in my letter not to associate with immoral people; I did not at all mean with the immoral
people of this world, or with the covetous and
swindlers, or with idolaters; for then you would
have to go out of the world. But actually, I wrote
to you not to associate with any so-called brother if
he should be an immoral person, or covetous, or an
idolater, or a reviler, or a drunkard, or a swindler—
not even to eat with such a one. For what have I
to do with judging outsiders? Do you not judge
those who are within the church? But those who are
outside, God judges. Remove the wicked man from
among yourselves" (1 Cor. 5:9-13).

3. *Facing the judgment of God.* The most serious
result of sexual sin is the fact that we must face the
judgment of God. The Bible is quite clear about this
matter. "and that no man transgress and defraud his
brother in the matter because the Lord is the aven-
ger in all these things, just as we also told you before and solemnly warned you" (1 Thess. 4:6). The
Lord's judgment may be experienced in this life, as
well as in the life to come. If we do not judge ourselves (1 Cor. 11:31), then we can expect the judgment of God to come at some point.

"Now the deeds of the flesh are evident, which
are: immorality, impurity, sensuality, idolatry, sor-
cery, enmities, strife, jealousy, outbursts of anger,
disputes, dissensions, factions, envyings, drunken-
ness, carousings, and things like these, of which I
forewarn you just as I have forewarned you that
those who practice such things shall not inherit the
kingdom of God" (Ga. 5:19-21). To put it another
way, if we continue in sin without repentance, the
Bible teaches that we will not be saved—and in fact,
are not saved, no matter what we claim before

others.

The results of sensuality are obviously serious. "For this you know with certainty, that no immoral or impure person or covetous man, who is an idolater, has an inheritance in the kingdom of Christ and God" (Eph. 5:5).

"But for the cowardly and unbelieving and abominable and murderers and immoral persons and sorcerers and idolaters and all liars, their part will be in the lake that burns with fire and brimstone, which is the second death" (Rev. 21:8). A narcissistic culture does not want to hear about God's evaluations or predicted punishments. Again, ours is an Epicurean age: "Eat, drink, and be merry, for tomorrow we die." But God says "it is appointed for men to die once, and after this comes judgment" (Heb. 9:27).

The promotion of sensualism is big business. Its marketing techniques pervade our society. One cannot escape its deadly suggestiveness nor the fragrance of its alluring perfumes. It captures the heart of multitudes because it is presented in such attractive forms. Christians, who should realize the dangers, are often caught in the web of these constant allurements. Where commitment to God is lacking, defeat is guaranteed.

A Place to Begin

If you or some of your close friends are struggling with the problems of sensuality, the big question is how to stop. How can a person overcome the constant pressure and temptations to be sexually involved with others outside of marriage? With so many people saying that there is nothing wrong with it, a person's level of resistance is often weakened. What do you do if you really want to please God and stop the wrong use of sex?

First, confess your sin to God. Don't try to ignore this basic step. God already knows what you are doing or have done. He doesn't need the information, but you need to admit it before Him. If the Bible calls it sin, then that's what it is. Admit it before God as the first step to victory.

Second, recognize your need of God's power through the ministry of the Holy Spirit who indwells every believer. Many people make the mistake of relying on their own ingenuity or inward strength to resist temptation. Galatians 5:16 says, "Walk by the Spirit, and you will not carry out the desire of the flesh." The Holy Spirit has been given to you to help you control your sinful desires. We are to *walk* (the word suggests a step-by-step process) in obedience to what He wants, trusting His power. Where do we find out what He wants? In the Bible. What God says in its pages will help us overcome sinful desires.

Third, confess and seek the forgiveness of anyone against whom you have sinned. Often, the peace of God is lacking in our hearts because we have not done this. Is there someone with whom you have had sex and to whom you have failed to apologize and ask forgiveness? If that person is a temptation for you to talk to by phone or be with in person, then write a letter.

Fourth, analyze the process that has led you to sin sexually and avoid all the steps in the sequence of temptation. Paul told Timothy, "Flee youthful lusts" (2 Tim. 2:22). Don't get close. Don't trust your ability to overcome the temptation. Do what God says and stay far from it (as much as is humanly possible).

Fifth, believe and rely on God's forgiveness. Christians often doubt that God has forgiven them (sometimes this results from our inability to forgive ourselves). The cross of Jesus Christ finished the work of redemption. Our task is to believe in what Jesus has done for us already, not in our ability to do what is right. "If we confess our sins, He is faithful and righteous to forgive us our sins and to cleanse us from all unrighteousness" (1 Jn. 1:9).

Those words are a tremendous promise. Cling to them and don't let anyone convince you otherwise.

Chapter 7

The Joys of Evangelism

TODAY (AS I WRITE THIS) I had the joy of introducing a person to faith in Jesus Christ. It was a time when I was tired and emotionally drained. I really didn't want to talk with anyone, but this man's sister had asked me to see him. Joe was heavily involved with drug addiction; his life was miserable and he wanted help. After getting acquainted, I told Joe the story of the gospel, how Jesus Christ died for our sins and rose again from the dead. His eyes lit up and tears rolled down his cheeks as he heard me describe God's love and forgiveness. He could hardly believe that such things could be true. We prayed, and he asked Jesus Christ to come into his life and save him.

No matter how often I have witnessed someone's response to the Lord, it is still a joy to see. My whole attitude changed. My problems seemed small. My focus was now off myself and onto this new baby in Christ.

Introspection and frequent discussions with others about our own feelings and needs don't lead us toward evangelism. When our thoughts turn inward, there is little outward concern for those who aren't in God's family. Many people assume that if we just can get our own act together, then we'll care about the needs of others. The truth is, however, the opposite is often the case. The more concerned we are about ourselves, the less concerned we are about eternal issues and the destiny of those without Christ.

Evangelism is a matter of pleasing God. "Whether, then, you eat or drink or whatever you do, do all to the glory of God. Give no offense either to Jews or to Greeks or to the church of God; just as I also please all men in all things, not seeking my own profit, but the profit of the many, that they may be saved" (1 Cor. 10:31-33).

When Paul taught that all we do should bring glory to God, he went on to apply that concept to evangelism. God is glorified when we stop seeking our own interests ("profit"), but rather seek to "please all men in all things." Many Christians have never really understood that. Trying to "please" other people, especially if they are unbelievers, seems like a contradiction, if not a compromise. "Separation" (although a biblical doctrine under some circumstances) has been taught to the point of our being isolated from unbelievers, the very ones God has called us to reach for Him.

Ask yourself this question: Am I seeking to please unbelievers in order to win them to Christ and bring glory to God? If so, what does that mean in practical terms?

In 1 Corinthians 9, Paul discussed the importance of our commitment to evangelism. After establishing the right of God's servants to receive material support for proclaiming the gospel (vv. 1-14) he then laid out four major principles that must characterize the person who desires to please God by winning others to Christ.

1. *Proper attitudes*—1 Corinthians 9:15-18. But I have used none of these things. And I am not writing these things that it may be done so in my case; for it would be better for me to die than have any man make my boast an empty one. For if I preach the gospel, I have nothing to boast of, for I am under compulsion; for woe is me if I do not preach the gospel. For if I do this voluntarily, I have a reward; but if against my will, I have a stewardship entrusted to me. What then is my reward? That, when I preach the gospel, I may offer the gospel without charge, so as not to make full use of my right in the gospel.

The proper attitude needed for proclaiming the gospel to nonbelievers is to be faithful to the gospel regardless of any personal benefit or support. Paul argued in the opening verses of this chapter that missionaries had a right to financial support, along with their responsibility to preach, a stewardship (v. 17) entrusted to them. Their reward would come from God, and even if no support were given, they were to be faithful in speaking out the truth of the gospel. Our witness, too, to nonbelievers should never be based on the personal benefit or support we may or may not receive. The proclamation of the gospel should not be based on any motive other than the salvation of others.

2. *Spiritual aims*—1 Corinthians 9:19, 22. Those who please God and bring glory to Him in their contact and association with nonbelievers have one great spiritual aim: "For though I am free from all men, I have made myself a slave to all, that I might win the more. . . . I have become all things to all men, that I may by all means save some." That as many people as possible be won to faith in Jesus Christ as Lord and Savior is to be a serious concern of all believers.

Having said that, we of course must recognize other priorities and responsibilities as well: marriage, family, use of spiritual gifts, work, prayer, Bible study, fellowship with other believers, etc. It is difficult to be "in balance." But if we say it pleases God when the gospel is proclaimed to nonbelievers, we must each evaluate when we intend to do that— and how.

Most Christians would agree that one of their goals in life is to win others to Christ. But when do we accomplish that goal? Is it really a goal of ours if its results can never be measured? To have an aim to win nonbelievers to faith in Christ is wonderful, but it doesn't tell us much about how we go about doing it. If we set a prayer goal this year to share the gospel with ten people, whose names we record along with the times we have spoken to them about Christ, then we have something that can be accomplished and evaluated.

Spiritual aims obviously should be backed up with prayer. What do we intend to do in order to accomplish the lofty and admirable objectives we have for ourselves as Christians? That's where it gets difficult: to *do* something about what we say are our objectives in life.

Those who desire to please God will realize that our aim will control what we do. Our contacts with nonbelievers will become much more exciting and meaningful when we understand that a spiritual aim controls why we are going to associate with them and what we are going to say. Paul clearly taught that we are to associate with nonbelievers (1 Cor. 5:9-10). Jesus was committed to "seek and to save that which was lost" (Lk. 19:10), and that commitment governed His relationships with nonbelievers even though He was criticized for them. When tax-gatherers and others came to Jesus to listen to Him, "both the Pharisees and the scribes began to grumble, saying, 'This man receives sinners and eats with them'"(Lk. 15:1-2).

Many Christians will not do what Jesus did. Somehow we have concluded that association with nonbelievers is wrong and will lead us to sin. Although that may be so in certain cases, it does not have to happen. Christians should be able to associate with nonbelievers, seeking to "please" them in order to win them to Christ.

When our youngest son was beginning high school, he wanted to bring a non-Christian friend home to spend the weekend. He even asked us whether it was right to be a friend to him. We began to talk about evangelism. Of course it was okay.

That's what the Lord would want us to do. We were amused as well as proud to watch the way he handled this matter. He knew the boy used bad language, so he told him before he brought him into our house that we didn't swear. When we sat down at meal time, he told the boy that we prayed before our meals so "don't start to eat right away." He gave him a blow-by-blow analysis of what it means to live in a Christian home. At the time, my wife and I hoped he didn't scare him off. But the boy now claims to know the Lord as his Savior.

Although Christians should never try to shove the message of the gospel down anyone's throat, we are committed to making clear the good news that has changed our lives. We must pray that we will have the boldness to speak.

3. *Great adaptability*—1 Corinthians 9:20-22. A lot of Christians refuse to adapt to the lifestyle and interests of a nonbelieving friend. They are afraid they might become like that person or do the wrong things that he or she does. Now, if that adaptation means committing sin, then obviously we have to draw the line at that point. But if it means doing innocent things that the friend enjoys doing, then we should be willing to adapt at times even if we are not particularly attracted to that activity (or whatever it is).

Because the issue of our adaptability is somewhat subtle, it can be difficult to understand—or at least work out in real life. Most of us don't associate much with non-Christians because we have so little in common, so few similar interests. The thought that we should be willing to adapt in some ways seemingly does not occur to most believers who are protective of their relationships and fearful of unbelieving contacts. But Paul wrote:

> And to the Jews I became as a Jew, that I might win Jews; to those who are under the Law, as under the Law, though not being myself under the Law, that I might win those who are under the Law; to those who are without law, as without law, though not being without the law of God but under the law of Christ, that I might win those who are without law. To the weak I became weak, that I might win the weak; I have become all things to all men, that I may by all means save some.

How few of us seem to practice that. *Cultural adaptability* is an important principle among missionaries, who leave their own culture to live in another. Without the missionary's adaptability, very few persons of a different culture would be reached. What applies to missionaries who work in cross-cultural situations also applies to us in our contacts with nonbelievers.

Again, I don't mean compromising with sin. Paul said that he was not "without the law of God." He spoke about being under the "law of Christ," the law of love that causes us to adapt in order to win others to Christ. Do we try to "become all things" to all persons in order to facilitate their salvation? Are we even concerned "that they may be saved" (1 Cor. 10:33)? Is that our commitment? How far will we go in "pleasing" them? Or is our relationship to other Christians so all-consuming, so tight-knit, that we have little time for anyone else? As we all know, that can happen despite our best intentions. How to balance our time and efforts in the right way will require a lot of prayerful thought.

4. *Heavenly ambition*—1 Corinthians 9:24-27. Along with proper attitudes, spiritual aim, and great adaptability, we need heavenly ambition. A culture (even if Christian) that pleases itself will not be motivated by heavenly ambition. Consider Paul's argument in these verses:

> Do you not know that those who run in a race all run, but only one receives the prize? Run in such a way that you may win. And everyone who competes in the games exercises self-control in all things. They then do it to receive a perishable wreath, but we an imperishable. Therefore I run in such a way, as not without aim; I box in such a way, as not beating the air; but I buffet my body and make it my slave, lest possibly, after I have preached to others, I myself should be disqualified.

First, it is important to remember the context of evangelism in which those words were written. Second, heavenly ambition means that we desire to receive God's commendation much more than human approval. But, third, the aim of winning others to Christ will not be accomplished by those who are undisciplined. Here Paul gives at least three characteristics of the undisciplined believer. He or she is (*a*) lacking in direction—"without aim"; (*b*) Lacking in results—"beating the air"; (*c*) Lacking in self-control—"I buffet my body and make it my slave."

Our entire Christian culture must awaken to the world's need for evangelism. So few believers genuinely care about the lives of those without Christ. Among ourselves we may verbally express such concern, but we do little in actuality to reach our nonbelieving friends. The truth is, I fear, that most believers don't even have any nonbelieving friends with whom they associate and whom they are trying to influence.

After I had taught on the subject of evangelism a few years ago, a woman confronted me with these words: "I have never had anything to do with my nonbelieving neighbors, because I thought we weren't supposed to associate with the world." She told me that not only had she not witnessed to them, she had never even spoken to them although they had lived in the same building for fifteen years!

When I explained to her that worldliness did not refer to our contacts with persons who need Christ, it was as though her whole life changed. Her perspective broadened and brightened. She began with an "Open House," invited her neighbors over, and was surprised at their responsiveness. They all seemed glad that someone in the neighborhood was taking some initiative. She then started regular coffee times one weekday morning for the wives. After several weeks she suggested a Bible study in her home one night a week. Shockingly again, ten neighbors responded and the group consistently averaged six people each week. Two years later God gave her the opportunity to lead two of the wives to Jesus Christ. A few months later their husbands and children were converted. She began to see her neighborhood radically transformed by the power of the gospel.

A Place to Begin

We all can start somewhere. There are all kinds of ways to put yourself in contact with nonbelievers. It might mean playing a round of golf or a racquetball game, joining a bowling league, inviting people to dinner, attending a concert. Community activities are one place to start; civic organizations are another.

Reach out to people. You'll be surprised at the response. Some will reject your invitation but others will be thrilled. So many people are lonely and need friends. Start building bridges of friendship wherever you go and wherever you can. Take the initiative. Smile and introduce yourself. Pray for God's direction and look for opportunities. God wants to use us much more than we want to be used.

Stop making excuses. It's time to start pleasing God and putting some purpose into your life that is beyond your own interests. If we pour our lives into others, we will reap unforeseeable blessings.

Chapter 8

The Art of Giving to Others

JOHN AND DEBBIE are a delight to know. There's something about them that's different. They're such a joy to be with. What they say makes you feel important and wanted. Whenever you have a need, John and Debbie are there to meet it. He and his wife are constantly giving themselves, their time, and their money to help other people. When I was hurting emotionally a few years back, John took me out for a cup of coffee. He didn't preach at me, he just listened and told me how much he appreciated me.

The apostle Paul knew some people like John and Debbie in a Roman colony called Philippi. When he was in prison in Rome, these people still cared and shared. Here's what Paul said to them in a let-

101

ter:

> But I rejoiced in the Lord greatly, that now at last you have revived your concern for me; indeed, you were concerned before, but you lacked opportunity. Not that I speak from want; for I have learned to be content in whatever circumstances I am. I know how to get along with humble means, and I also know how to live in prosperity; in any and every circumstance I have learned the secret of being filled and going hungry, both of having abundance and suffering need. I can do all things through Him who strengthens me. Nevertheless, you have done well to share with me in my affliction. And you yourselves also know, Philippians, that at the first preaching of the gospel, after I departed from Macedonia, no church shared with me in the matter of giving and receiving but you alone; for even in Thessalonica you sent a gift more than once for my needs. Not that I seek the gift itself, but I seek for the profit which increases to your account. But I have received everything in full, and have an abundance; I am amply supplied, having received from Epaphroditus what you have sent, a fragrant aroma, an acceptable sacrifice, well-pleasing to God. And my God shall supply all your needs according to His riches in glory in Christ Jesus. Now to our God and Father be the glory forever and ever" (Phil. 4:10-20).

The giving of these Philippian believers to Paul was "well-pleasing to God." When we get our eyes off ourselves and our own problems, we can begin to please God by serving and caring for others. Paul said this also to the leaders of the church in Ephesus, "In every thing I showed you that by working hard in this manner you must help the weak and remember the words of the Lord Jesus, that He Himself said, 'It is more blessed to give than to receive'" (Acts 20:35).

Do you believe that statement? Is it more blessed to give than to receive? Do you desire to receive, but spend little time giving? If so, you are heading for disappointment, discouragement, and defeat. It delights the heart of God when we care enough to give to others in need.

The theme of giving to others fills the Bible, and is specifically related to pleasing God in Hebrews 13:16: "And do not neglect doing good and sharing; for with such sacrifices God is pleased." The act of giving and sharing with others is "a fragrant aroma" to God. He accepts it as a sacrifice to Him (Phil. 4:18). In a sense, therefore, when we give to others we are giving to God and honoring Him.

Mrs. Jones used to be cynical and bitter about most things in life. Some people said she had always been that way. But one day her husband came to talk to me about all this negativism. He couldn't take it anymore; he wanted help.

In several subsequent sessions with her, one of our counselors discovered that her self-centeredness was eating her up. It turned out that that was like the attitude of her parents. She had grown up in a home with extremely critical parents. As a child she had learned how to attack others verbally and see the negative side of things.

Her life began to change rapidly when the counselor talked to her about the art of giving to others. She challenged Mrs. Jones to start giving without thought of receiving, to give even when there was no response from the recipients. It was not easy, but gradually, step by step, she began to do that. Today her husband and children praise her. A marvelous transformation has occurred in their home.

The Greek word for *grace* in the New Testament can also be translated "gift." Grace *gives*. It is not based on the merits of the one to whom something is given. That's why grace has been called the "unmerited favor" of God. God's grace gives to you when you don't deserve it, when you've done nothing to earn it. Because God is a God of grace, He is pleased when graciousness characterizes what we do, and the way we are, in our relationships with other people.

The word *grace* occurs 156 times in the New Testament, so it is no small subject. A form of the word, translated "gift," is used an additional seventeen times; and the verb form is used about twenty-three times. Grace has given us salvation and eternal life through the work of Jesus Christ. Grace abounds where sin is found; it is greater than our sin. Grace gives us all things through Christ our Lord (Rom. 8:32). Spiritual gifts are the result of God's grace (Rom. 12:6). Forgiveness and tenderheartedness are matters of God's grace. In Ephesians 4:32, the English words "forgiving" and "forgiven" are based on the Greek word for grace. When we forgive someone, we demonstrate grace to them; we give them what they may not deserve.

God's grace is sufficient for our every need (2 Cor. 12:9). He invites us to come to His "throne of grace" where we will find grace to help us in time of need (Heb. 4:16). God's grace is given to the humble, not to the proud, self-sufficient person (Jms. 4:6; 1 Pet. 5:5). We are to grow in grace (2 Pet. 3:18) and show grace to others (Heb. 12:28—"let us show gratitude").

A songwriter, Julia H. Johnston (1849-1919), wrote these beautiful words about God's grace:

Marvelous grace of our loving Lord,
Grace that exceeds our sin and our guilt!
Yonder on Calvary's mount outpoured -
There where the blood of the Lamb was spilt.

Sin and despair, like the sea-waves cold,
Threaten the soul with infinite loss;
Grace that is greater - yes, grace untold -
Points to the Refuge, the mighty cross.

Dark is the stain that we cannot hide,
What can avail to wash it away?
Look! there is flowing a crimson tide -
Whiter than snow you may be today.

Marvelous, infinite, matchless grace,
Freely bestowed on all who believe!
You that are longing to see His face,
Will you this moment His grace receive?

CHORUS:
Grace, grace, God's grace,
Grace that will pardon and cleanse within;
Grace, grace, God's grace,
Grace that is greater than all our sin!

Our personal worthiness is not the issue. We have done nothing to deserve or earn God's favor. Rather, he gives to us on the basis of His love and forgiveness, and we must learn to be like that with others. When we are, it pleases God—because that reflects His character. He wants His children to be people of grace, constantly giving to others what they don't necessarily deserve.

The Blessings of Giving

Why give? Many Bible passages answer that question.

1. *Giving pleases God*—Heb. 13:16; Phil. 4:18. When we please God, we are fulfilling the basic purpose of our creation and existence. Giving accomplishes that, and thus is a way to honor and dedicate our lives to our Lord.

2. *Giving meets the needs of others*—Phil. 4:10-20. Paul told the Philippian Christians how their gifts had met his needs on various occasions. Earlier, Paul had collected an offering for Jews living in Judea who were experiencing famine and persecution.

But now, I am going to Jerusalem serving the saints. For Macedonia and Achaia have been pleased to make a contribution for the poor among the saints in Jerusalem. Yes, they were pleased to do so, and they are indebted to them. For if the Gentiles have shared in their spiritual things, they are indebted to minister to them also in material things. Therefore, when I have finished this, and have put my seal on this fruit of theirs, I will go on by way of you to Spain. And I know that when I come to you, I will come in the fulness of the blessing of Christ (Rom. 15:25-29).

What caused these Gentile believers to give help to the poor in Jerusalem? Paul said it resulted from the "grace of God which has been given in the churches of Macedonia" (2 Cor. 8:1).

. . . in a great ordeal of affliction their abundance of joy and their deep poverty overflowed in the wealth of their liberality. For I testify that according

according to their ability, and beyond their ability
they gave of their own accord, begging us with
much entreaty for the favor of participation in the
support of the saints, and this, not as we had ex-
pected, but they first gave themselves to the Lord
and to us by the will of God (2 Cor. 8:2-5).

The key is found in the phrase, "they first gave
themselves to the Lord." True giving starts with personal commitment of your life to God. We are stew-
ards, not owners, of all that God has given to us.
Great blessings result as we seek to minister to
others and meet their needs.

3. *Giving provides for your own needs*—2 Cor. 9:8-
10; Phil. 4:19. When you give to others, God promises to supply your needs as well. "And my God
shall supply all your needs according to His riches
in glory in Christ Jesus." That's God's promise.

And God is able to make all grace abound to you,
that always having all sufficiency in everything, you
may have an abundance for every good deed; as it
is written, "He scattered abroad, He gave to the
poor, His righteousness abides forever." Now He
who supplies seed to the sower and bread for food
will supply and multiply your seed for sowing and
increase the harvest of your righteousness.

God promises to supply all your need. He is the
great Supplier, and He will honor you when you
seek to help others in their time of need.

4. *Giving causes people to give thanks to God*—2
Cor. 9:11-13. When we give to others, we are giving
those people a reason to praise the Lord.

You will be enriched in everything for all liberality,

which through us is producing thanksgiving to God. For the ministry of this service is not only fully supplying the needs of the saints, but is also overflowing through many thanksgivings to God. Because of the proof given by this ministry they will glorify God for your obedience to your confession of the gospel of Christ, and for the liberality of your contribution to them and to all.

When we give to others, they in turn give thanks to God. He has supplied their needs through you. The art of giving to others is rooted in our desire to bring glory and thanks to God.

5. *Giving increases your own productivity*—2 Cor. 9:6. Although we don't want to slip back into self-promoting activities or selfish ambition, we must also recognize that giving to others brings with it many promises of increased productivity. "Now this I say, he who sows sparingly shall also reap sparingly; and he who sows bountifully shall also reap bountifully."

The "sowing" in this context deals with giving to the poor in Jerusalem. Here is a promise of increased productivity based on the amount of sowing. A similar thought is found in the book of Proverbs: "Honor the LORD from your wealth, And from the first of all your produce; So your barns will be filled with plenty, And your vats will overflow with new wine" (3:9-10).

My wife and I have experienced the truth of this concept on many occasions. A couple to whom we were close in the past was going through some financial difficulties, so we decided to send them a check. Through the next several months we continued to encourage and support them financially. Several years later this couple blessed us with some financial help that took us completely by surprise. It was so much more than we had given them. Once again it illustrated God's principle to us.

When an attitude of joyous giving characterizes you, God seems to increase your ability to give and be a continued blessing. When your attitude is that of getting something in return, it won't work. God cannot be fooled or manipulated. When the self enters the picture for any reason, the blessing of God is hindered.

One of the Bible's great statements about the blessing of God in giving is found in God's instruction to Israel concerning the tithe for the storehouse (the temple).

"Will a man rob God? Yet you are robbing Me! But you say, 'How have we robbed Thee?' In tithes and contributions. You are cursed with a curse, for you are robbing Me, the whole nation of you! Bring the whole tithe into the storehouse, so that there may be food in My house, and test Me now in this," says the Lord of hosts, "if I will not open for you the windows of heaven, and pour out for you a blessing until there is no more need" (Mal. 3:8-10).

What a promise God gave to His people Israel. He is a God who wants to bless us far more than we want to receive it. The New Testament contains a similar promise. Jesus taught, "Give, and it will be given to you; good measure, pressed down, shaken together, running over, they will pour into your lap. For whatever measure you deal out to others, it will be dealt to you in return" (Lk. 6:38).

Are we truly pleasing God by how and what we

give? Or is *self* still controlling our funds and resources? Let's let go of the controls and learn to
share.

A Place to Begin

If you really want to learn the art of giving,
here's a way to start. Write down your total income
on the top of a piece of paper. Next, list your
monthly expenses. (If there's more expense than income, it's time to make some changes.) Then take
the amount left over and divide into the following
categories:

25% - give to your local church
25% - give to the support of missionaries
10% - put into savings or investments
5% - use for family fun or recreation
10% - give to people in need

For the sake of illustration, suppose your total
income is $30,000 a year, and your expenses are
$20,000. That leaves you $10,000 to divide up: $2,500
to your local church; $2,500 to missionaries; $1,000
into savings; $500 for fun or recreation; and $1,000
to people in need. I guarantee that you will have
great joy in giving away that $1,000.

Chapter 9

Submission to Authority

MY WIFE AND I were having breakfast in a local restaurant, a favorite weekly custom with us, when we noticed a young mother with a small child in the next booth. The child was in a high chair and was throwing food on the floor. The mother kept saying, "Please don't do that." After repeated efforts to stop the child, all of which failed, she said at the top of her voice, "Will you please stop doing that!" The child looked straight at her and said, "NO!" After that, that mother simply gave in to her child's wishes, however embarrassing it was. I had all I could do to keep from going over to that kid and delivering a well-placed slap to his little rear end!

But it reminded me that we adults often act like that little child. We too are unsubmissive to authority. We live in a permissive environment, and unless we had parents who knew the meaning of discipline, and administered it with wisdom and love, the chances are we will be submissive also.

The *self* by its very nature is unsubmissive. It refuses to bend. It demands its own rights; it wants its own way. It rarely looks at the viewpoint of others; much less is it willing to submit to the authority of others.

Today there is a crisis of authority in our culture. Who's in charge anyway? And does anyone respect persons in authority? We have lost confidence in authority figures, understandably. Our politicians have often been less than the ideal envisions. Cheating, bribery, manipulation, lying, stealing: all exemplify wrong values and deteriorating integrity, and we have seen those vices too often among people whose lives should be exemplary.

Our culture has been saturated with secular humanism. By that, I mean a philosophy that sees human beings as captains of their fate and regards the quality of human relationships as the only criterion of what is right and wrong. Humanism tells us that we can't let anyone tell us what to do. Let people know you won't be shoved around. Who cares what others think? Humanism teaches you to think of yourself first.

That outlook centers, I believe, in the absence of respect and fear of God Almighty. Secular humanism has no room for God. It either ignores Him or denies His existence and relevance. When the foundation of morality and authority is removed, respect for authority stands on shaky ground. Who has a right to tell us what is right and wrong?

Yet our legal system is based on certain accepted standards of morality that originally assumed the presence of God and a revelation of certain moral standards. Where does law come from? Who has a right to say? Is authority determined only by military might? Is submission possible only when looking at the barrel of a gun or the threat of attack?

The Basis of All Authority

The apostle Paul wrote, "Let every person be in subjection to the governing authorities. For there is no authority except from God, and those which exist are established by God" (Rom. 13:1). How simple it sounds. God Himself is the foundation. Whatever we mean by the word *authorities*, He established. If there is such a thing as parental authority, then God established it. If there is political authority, then God is in back of it. We are to be in subjection to all positions of authority. Romans 13:2 says, "He who resists authority has opposed the ordinance of God."

When people fail to recognize God's authority behind all positions of human authority, they set themselves up as the authority. They make the decisions whether or not to submit.

God has set up certain levels of authority for human beings. They include *marriage*, which places the position of authority on the shoulders of the husband; the *family*, with the parents acting as authorities; *government*, with its many officials and rulers; *business*, with employers acting in a role of authority over employees; and the *church*, with its leaders entrusted with the responsibility to manage its affairs. These levels of authority exist because God has established them. Society and human relationships suffer when God's authority structure is not maintained.

Why Submit to Authority?

The Bible teaches that submission to authority pleases God. If our desire were truly centered in the glory and pleasure of God, it would be easy for us to submit to authority.

The morality behind our submission is important to understand. We obey because it is right to do so. It doesn't matter whether I feel like it or whether I have a reason for it. I am to submit because it is the right thing to do; it pleases God, supposedly the major objective of my life.

The matter of obedience is emphasized in 1 John 3:22—"And whatever we ask we receive from Him, because we keep His commandments and do the things that are pleasing in His sight." Obedience to authority is an act that demonstrates we are living our lives to the glory of God.

Selfish ambition, however, does not enjoy submission. It fights against it. The self wants to be in control, to assert its rights and desires. "The mind set on the flesh is hostile toward God; for it does not subject itself to the law of God, for it is not even able to do so; and those who are in the flesh cannot please God" (Rom. 8:7-8).

That's the problem. Selfishness (or carnality) does not respond to God's laws. Paul says that it cannot do so, nor is it able to please God.

The Art of Submission

Obedience is not easy to understand or apply. We have a natural tendency to question every demand on our time, resources, and energies. We want reasons. We want to maintain our independence. We struggle against submission.

The word *obedience* in the New Testament is represented by at least three Greek words.

1. A word that means "to arrange under." This military term, often referring to rank, is used forty times as a verb and four times as a noun. It is the word in Romans 13:1 when God instructs every person to be "in subjection to the governing authorities." It is the word used for wives being in subjection to their husbands (1 Tim. 2:11; 1 Cor. 14:34; Eph. 5:22; Col. 3:18; Tit. 2:5; 1 Pet. 3:1, 5). It is the word when younger men are instructed to be submissive to older men (1 Pet. 5:5). It is used of the parent/child relationship (1 Tim. 3:4). Jesus Christ was an example of such submission (Lk. 2:51). He was always pleasing to God, including being obedient to his parents.

Servants are to be in subjection to their masters (Tit. 2:9; 1 Pet. 2:18). Believers are to be subject to one another (Eph. 5:21). All things have been put in subjection to the authority of Jesus Christ (1 Cor. 15: 27; Eph. 1:22; Heb. 2:8; 1 Pet. 3:22).

2. A word that means "to listen under." This word implies specific response to authority: hearing or listening and then responding to what was said. It appears twenty-one times as a verb and fifteen times as a noun. It is used of the obedience of chil-

dren to their parents (Eph. 6:1; Col. 3:20). It is used of servants to their masters (Eph. 6;5; Col. 3:22). It is also used in a New Testament reference to Sarah obeying Abraham (1 Pet. 3:6)

When the Bible speaks about becoming believers through obeying the Word of God, this word is chosen (Acts 6:7; Rom. 6:17; Heb. 5:9). We might use the English word *hearken* though the word is usually translated "obedience."

3. A word that means "to obey one in authority." The verb includes the word *persuade* as well as the word for "ruler." It was used when Peter and the apostles said, "We must *obey* God rather than men" (Acts 5:29) and later in the same chapter: "And we are witnesses of these things; and so is the Holy Spirit, whom God has given to those who obey Him" (Acts 5:32). Again, "Remind them to be subject to rulers, to authorities, to be *obedient*, to be ready for every good deed" (Tit. 3:1).

A young man discussing his family problems with me a few years ago was not getting what he hoped to hear. This rebellious young man was trying to present arguments as to why he didn't need to obey his parents. One, they were unbelievers; two, his dad was an alcoholic and, in the son's mind, didn't deserve any respect. Three, their advice was usually wrong and not in line with biblical teachings. Four, they had never accepted him or responded properly to him since his decision to become a Christian. He felt he had just reasons for not responding to their authority.

When I explained that the Bible's teaching about submission was not just for believers to believers, but also for believers to unbelievers, he seemed surprised. It was as though I had removed his grounds for rebellion. I challenged him to regard his parents as the authorities in his life and to pray daily for their salvation. I encouraged him to recognize that God would use his submission to them as a tool in reaching them for Christ. In this case, that teenager was wise and responded willingly. His attitude changed, and within a few months his parents visited our church to see what had made such a difference in their son. Eventually they too received Christ and, to this day, they credit their son's submissive attitude toward them as the key that brought them to the Lord.

Submission Takes Humility

James 4:7 says, "Submit therefore to God." And in verse 10: "Humble yourselves in the presence of the Lord, and He will exalt you." Whenever you think you are smarter, wiser, and more capable than the person in authority over you (it may be true), your spirit will resist being submissive.

One businessman told me about his struggles with submission. His immediate supervisor was a man for whom he had no respect. This businessman felt far more capable of managing the department in which he worked. The man over him was blunt, crude, and often offensive to the women in the office. This Christian businessman not only resented his authority, but found himself agreeing with others in the office and joining in their verbal attacks.

On the way to work one day, he was listening to a Christian radio station. The preacher was dealing with humility. This man, convicted, began to realize that he was not pleasing God by criticizing his superior and withholding respect from him. To make a long story short, he eventually had the joy of leading his boss to Christ because of the enormous change in attitude that took place in his heart that day. Further, his humility and kindness began to affect everyone in the office.

The Bible teaches that Moses, although a great leader, was extraordinarily humble. "Now the man Moses was very humble, more than any man who was on the face of the earth" (Num. 11:3). On one occasion when his sister Miriam and his brother Aaron demonstrated an unsubmissive attitude toward his authority, Moses refused to seek revenge. God, however, honored his humility and brought His own revenge. Moses was able to exercise great authority over others because he himself was submissive to God's authority.

Should We Ever Refuse to Submit?

There are times when we must refuse to be submissive to man's authority. Hebrews 11:23-27 tells us some of the reasons why Moses was honored by God. His submission to God was evident by what he refused to do as well as by what he chose to do. Pleasures and money did not capture his heart; rather, obedience to God did. Moses kept his eyes on the Lord, not fearing those who tempted him or tried to persecute him. His trust and confidence were in the Lord.

When our submission to God conflicts with our submission to human authority, we must draw the line. Obedience to God comes first. If God says that something is morally wrong, it is wrong, and we must refuse to do it even though human leaders order us to do otherwise.

A good case in point is that of Peter and John in Acts 5. The Sanhedrin (ruling body of the Jewish people in ancient times) said to these men: "We gave you strict orders not to continue teaching in this name, and behold, you have filled Jerusalem with your teaching, and intend to bring this man's blood upon us" (Acts 5:28). However, Jesus had instructed His disciples to preach and teach to all the nations of the world. That was His command—and His authority was certainly higher than that of the Sanhedrin! So, Peter and the apostles answered in Acts 5:29: "We must obey God rather than men."

In spite of the beating they received and the order to speak no more in the name of Jesus (Acts 5:40), the apostles left with joy in their hearts that they were counted worthy by God to suffer for the name of Jesus. Acts 5:42 says: "And every day, in the temple and from house to house, they kept right on teaching and preaching Jesus as the Christ."

Dr. Robert Wells, a respected physician, serves in obstetrics and gynecology in Long Beach, California. A few years ago, he was involved, like so many other doctors, in performing abortions. Today, because of his faith in Jesus Christ and his understanding of what the Bible teaches about the sanctity of human life, he refuses to perform any abortions. He has submitted to a higher authority—the authority of God Himself.

One lady's husband wanted her to have an abortion. She disobeyed his wishes because she believed it was morally wrong. Her submission to God required her to refuse to submit to her husband. There are times when we must disobey man in order to obey God.

A teenage boy asked me one day if God would forgive him if he lied. It seems his father was asking him to lie about several important matters, and it was deeply troubling this young man. I told him that it was always wrong to lie, and that his submission to God was more important than his submission to his father.

Life is filled with such problems, and we must often make a choice. To please God, we must be submissive to authority, but it certainly does not please God when we violate His authority in order to submit to some human authority. How we need the wisdom of God in these matters. Because many Christians argued for submission to the government no matter what that government did, millions of people in Germany lost their lives during the Nazi regime under Hitler. There is a time when it is morally right to disobey human authority in order to be submissive to God and to please Him in all we do and say.

The Example of Christ

Jesus said, "Behold, I have come to do Thy will, O God" (Heb. 10:7). The Gospel of John records these words from the lips of our Lord: "I always do the things that are pleasing to Him" (8:29). In no area was Jesus' example of pleasing God more powerful than in his willing submission to His heavenly Father.

One particular incident that demonstrates Jesus'

submission to authority is the night He spent in the garden of Gethsemane. The Bible says that He prayed: "Father, if Thou art willing, remove this cup from Me; yet not My will, but Thine be done" (Lk. 22:42). He was "in agony" and was praying "very fervently" (v. 44). His sweat "became like drops of blood, falling down upon the ground."

Hebrews 5:7-9 makes these comments on this incident in the garden: "In the days of His flesh, He offered up both prayers and supplications with loud crying and tears to Him who was able to save Him from death, and who was heard because of His piety, although He was a Son, He learned obedience from the things which He suffered; and having been made perfect, He became to all those who obey Him the source of eternal salvation." Our Lord was an example of submission to authority, of absolute obedience, even to death on the cross (Phil. 2:8). God was so pleased that He "highly exalted Him, and bestowed on Him the name which is above every name" (Phil. 2:9).

The example of Christ moved songwriter Mary D. James to write this stanza in her hymn "All for Jesus":

Since my eyes were fixed on Jesus,
I've lost sight of all beside,
So enchained my spirit's vision,
Looking at the Crucified.

If only we would keep our eyes on the example of Jesus, we would have fewer questions about how to respond to authority in our lives. His example of submission (1 Pet. 2:21-25) was the basis for Peter's admonition to wives: "In the same way [as Jesus Christ], you wives, be submissive to your own husbands so that even if any of them are disobedient to the word, they may be won without a word by the behavior of their wives, as they observe your chaste and respectful behavior" (1 Pet. 3:1-2).

But note this: Jesus' submission is also an example for husbands to demonstrate a submissive attitude toward the needs of their wives. "You husbands likewise [as Jesus Christ], live with your wives in an understanding way, as with a weaker vessel, since she is a woman; and grant her honor as a fellow-heir of the grace of life, so that your prayers may not be hindered" (1 Pet. 3:7).

A Place to Begin

Submission to one another is what really pleases God. Though we wrestle with its implications on a day-to-day basis, let us never underestimate its importance.

Who are the authorities in your present life? Can you think of ways that your attitude toward them needs improvement?

Chapter 10

Learning to Praise God

WHEN WE FOCUS ON ourselves, we rarely praise God for anything. If we see most of life as a series of circumstances that we ourselves must handle, we find little cause to praise God. Clearly the "age of self" has drawn our hearts away from God. We even go to church to be "ministered to," if not entertained. It's time, I think, to get our priorities straight.

Praising God is a part of why we were created in the first place. "Through Him then, let us continually offer up a sacrifice of praise to God, that is, the fruit of lips that give thanks to His name" (Heb. 13:15). Verse 16 says, "with such sacrifices God is pleased." We please God, therefore, when we praise Him verbally, orally. "I will praise the name of God with song, And shall magnify Him with thanksgiving. And it will please the LORD better than an ox, Or a young bull with horns and hoofs" (Ps. 69:30-31). God is pleased with the "sacrifice of praise and thanksgiving" to His name. When we exalt God for who He is and what He can do, He is pleased.

Many psalms have the praise of God as their theme. "I will sing to the Lord as long as I live; I will sing praise to my God while I have my being. Let my meditation be pleasing to Him; As for me, I shall be glad in the Lord" (Ps. 104:33-34). Singing to the Lord, offering praise and thanksgiving to His name, comes from a heart that knows why it exists. We were designed to praise His holy name.

The need for Christians and churches who praise God is great in our generation. Recently, I sense, there has been a slight change in the format of service of some evangelical churches, a shift toward the worship and praise of God. It's about time. Church services that seem more like entertainment than anything else have characterized the past few decades of evangelical ministry. The focus, like that of our culture, has been on the needs of people. Not that there is anything wrong with ministering to people's needs. The problem centers in what has been left out, the worship and praise of God. Seminarians have been told that effective preaching is preaching that deals with human need, and of course that is true. Yet without the worship of God, our preaching is less than what God intends. All ministry must begin with the objective of worshiping God. He comes first. Everything else is second, no matter how important it may be. All is to be done to the glory of God.

What did Jesus have to say about worship? "But an hour is coming, and now is, when the true worshipers shall worship the Father in spirit and truth; for such people the Father seeks to be His worshipers. God is spirit, and those who worship Him must worship in spirit and truth" (Jn. 4:23-24).

God the Father is seeking worshipers. Where are they?

What is Worship?

Does worship mean the use of candles, robes, and altars? Does it require stained-glass windows and other religious symbolism? Is it ritual, a certain order of events, in a church service?

When speaking of worship, the New Testament uses a word meaning "to kiss toward." It is used as a verb sixty times, and once as a noun in John 4:23. The wise men came to worship Jesus (Mt. 2:11). Certain other individuals also came to Jesus to worship Him. One was a leper (Mt. 8:2); another a synagogue official (Mt. 9:18). The disciples worshiped Jesus when He calmed the sea, saying "You are certainly God's Son" (Mt. 14:33). A Canaanite woman worshiped Him, asking Him to heal her demon-possessed daughter, which He did (Mt. 15:25). The mother of the sons of Zebedee worshiped Jesus and then asked for a special position for her sons in the kingdom of God (Mt. 20:22ff.). A man who lived among the tombs, possessed by an unclean spirit that severely tormented him, came to Jesus and worshiped Him, crying out for healing. He was delivered by Jesus' power when the demons were cast out (Mk. 5:2-20).

After Jesus' resurrection, certain women worshiped Him, grabbing His feet and holding on
tightly (Mt. 28:9). The eleven disciples worshiped
Him on a mountain in Galilee after His resurrection
even though some of them were doubtful (Mt.
28:17).

In the book of Hebrews, the Father said concerning His Son, "And let the angels of God worship Him" (1:6). An angel refused to allow the apostle John to worship him, but rather told him to
"worship God" (Rev. 22:8-9). Only God is to be worshiped, not human beings, not angels. Since God's
Son, Jesus, is to be worshiped, we conclude that He
is the eternal God in human flesh, the God-man.

The word for *worship* is often translated by the
New American Standard Bible as "bow down." To
bow down before God implies our recognition of His
greatness and sovereignty over all. It is to humble
ourselves in His presence. When Paul prayed, he
said, "I bow my knees before the Father" (Eph.
3:14). That is worship. It is God's will that "every
knee should bow, of those who are in heaven, and
on earth, and under the earth" (Phil. 2:10). Worship
of Jesus Christ is said to result in "the glory of God
the Father" (v. 11).

Worship also implies our realization of who we
are in the light of who God is. Isaiah the prophet
was hard hit by the impact of this distinction when
he had a vision of the Lord.

In the year of King Uzziah's death, I saw the Lord
sitting on a throne, lofty and exalted, with the train
of His robe filling the temple. Seraphim stood above
Him, each having six wings; with two he covered

his face, and with two he covered his feet, and with two he flew. And one called out to another and said, "Holy, Holy, Holy, is the LORD of hosts, the whole earth is full of His glory." And the foundations of the thresholds trembled at the voice of him who called out, while the temple was filling with smoke. Then I said, "Woe is me, for I am ruined! Because I am a man of unclean lips, and I live among a people of unclean lips; For my eyes have seen the King, the LORD of hosts" (Is. 6:1-5).

The sight of God on His throne caused Isaiah to realize his own and his people's sinfulness. True worship always involves that realization. God's greatness causes us to realize how unrighteous we are; were it not for His grace and compassion, we would be consumed (Lam. 3:22 KJV).

Worship is also our response to God for who He is and for what He has done and will do. Psalm 95 speaks eloquently of this:

O come, let us sing for joy to the LORD; Let us shout joyfully to the rock of our salvation. Let us come before His presence with thanksgiving; Let us shout joyfully to Him with psalms. For the LORD is a great God, And a great King above all gods, In whose hand are the depths of the earth; The peaks of the mountains are His also. The sea is His, for it was He who made it; And His hands formed the dry land. Come, let us worship and bow down; Let us kneel before the Lord our Maker. For He is our God, And we are the people of His pasture, and the sheep of His hand (vv. 1-7).

The Psalmist urged the people to sing and shout with much joy, to come before God with great thanksgiving and praise. Worship should be a joyful experience, according to the Bible, and singing is an important part of that. The somber silence of people in most churches today does not reflect scriptural teaching.

"Shout joyfully to the LORD, all the earth; Break forth and sing for joy and sing praises" (Ps. 98:4). "Shout joyfully to the LORD, all the earth. Serve the LORD with gladness; Come before Him with joyful singing" (Ps. 100:1-2). Worship is a joyful response of the heart toward the character and works of God. It is the result of our seeing Him properly, responding with fear, reverence, adoration, love, praise, thanksgiving.

Why Worship?

Once we have seen what worship is, the reasons for it should be clear. We are talking about the God who made us and designed us for His praise and adoration. But let's note the reasons we find in the Bible.

1. *We worship because God tells us to do it.* It is God's will that we should worship and praise Him (Rev. 22:9). Countless biblical passages emphasize this truth. That ought to settle it.

2. *We worship because the Father is seeking those who will worship Him.* The Father is looking for His creatures to worship Him (Jn. 4:23-24). His heart longs that we do so. Our worship pleases Him.

3. *We worship because the twenty-four elders in heaven do it.* Who are the twenty-four elders? Some say Israel. Some say angels. Some say Israel and the church. Others say the church in heaven, completed, and with the Lord during the tribulation on earth. It is possible that the twenty-four elders rep-

resent all the believers of past ages who have died and are now with the Lord. It is possible that the twenty-four elders represent the entire body of believers from Pentecost (Acts 2) until the rapture (1 Thess. 4:16-17).

"The twenty-four elders will fall down before Him who sits on the throne, and will worship Him who lives forever and ever, and will cast their crowns before the throne, saying, 'Worthy art Thou, our Lord and our God, to receive glory and honor and power; for Thou didst create all things, and because of Thy will they existed, and were created'"(Rev. 4:10-11). The twenty-four elders bowing down before God make clear what we will be doing forever and ever: we will be worshiping and praising God.

4. *We worship because God alone is worthy of such praise.* Worship is declaring the worth of God (Rev. 4:11; 5:9-14). It is extolling His virtues and attributes. It is exalting Him: declaring His marvelous works, and praising Him for all that He is doing now as well as for what He will do in the future.

How Do We Worship?

Churches exhibit radical differences in the form and format of worship. Each religious group has its own opinions about it. Because Christian worship varies in different countries and cultures, it's hard to separate principles of worship from our own background and current practices. What is cultural? What is essential? That is our continual problem.

All of us can agree that worship should be done from one's heart; we must, as Jesus taught, "worship the Father in spirit and truth." All the forms, symbols, and ceremonies that one may devise to encourage people to worship God does not mean that their hearts are truly responding to God.

God is not against art, beauty, or structure. One of the most beautiful buildings in the history of the world was the Jewish temple built by Solomon under God's direction. According to the New Testament, however, the temple of Solomon's day is now replaced by the sanctuary of our own bodies (1 Cor. 6:19-20). Does that fact rule out church buildings and beautiful architecture? People disagree. If buildings are an end in themselves, rather than the means to an end, then, of course, we are not properly motivated. If the teaching of the church implies that the buildings are the church, and not the people, then, once again, we have the wrong view.

On the other hand, the facilities in which we meet should not detract from the worship of God. We should not imply by how we build and design them that God is not interested in beauty and art. That is nowhere taught, and in some respects it is contradicted by the attitude of God toward His magnificent temple. It is hard to find the right balance. Buildings are not the main issue. They are like tools to be used. If the buildings encourage us to worship and praise our Lord, then God is honored. If they attract us to the point that the facilities are prominent and not the God whom they supposedly honor, then we have put too much into them.

Nor are robes essential. Neither are they unscriptural. Robes for the choir or the minister may help to direct our attention from personal attire and remind us that we are there to worship God. On the other hand, if such attire causes people to think that those who wear them are special, then it would be best to discard them. The priests of God's temple had marvelous attire, items of great beauty and attraction. But now all believers are priests (1 Pet. 2:9). Robes can foster an improper concept of ministry. They have a tendency to separate those "in front" from those "in the pew." It suggests a division between clergy and laity that is not intended by New Testament teaching. But robes in themselves are not moral items. It depends on how we relate to them.

Religious symbolism has existed throughout church history. Although some evangelical Christians today insist that they do not care for symbolism, the facts today prove otherwise. Fish symbols, dove symbols, cross symbols, etc., are found on our cars, books, brochures, pamphlets, necklaces, Bibles, shirts, hats—you name it, and we can probably put some symbol on it. Those things are not wrong in themselves, but they can be. They are not items to be worshiped. They are not "good luck charms." They will not increase our prayer life or make us better students of the Bible. We are not more spiritual because we wear them or display them.

What Are the Essentials of Worship?

If not buildings, art forms, symbols, candles, robes, stained-glass windows, etc., then what?

1. *Prayer.* We worship when we talk to God in thanksgiving, praise, adoration, confession, petition, etc. There is no worship without our personal communication with God, so we must talk to Him. Prayer is a priority in worship, not an option for a select few. Someone may lead us in prayer in

the public services of our churches, but those who lead should come before God on behalf of all the people, using the first person plural *we* and not the singular *I*.

Our times of prayer must be frequent. Small groups of believers who get together to pray should be encouraged. It is difficult to have everyone participate in large gatherings, but all of us can pray frequently in our hearts.

People must be taught to pray (remember that the disciples asked the Lord to teach them). People must see how prayer relates to worship. Prayer is not simply a "quickie" to God when you are in trouble (although He is always there, ready to hear and answer prayer). Small groups of Christians meeting for prayer during the week will enhance all the ministries of the church.

Prayer undergirds everything else; it is our most important ministry.

2. *Music.* We must grow up musically in this generation and recognize the importance of music in worshiping God. He encourages it. It pleases Him.

Psalm 81:1—"Sing for joy to God our strength"
Psalm 89:1—"I will sing of the lovingkindness of the LORD forever"
Psalm 92:1—"It is good . . . to sing praises to Thy name, O Most High"
Psalm 92:4—"I will sing for joy at the works of Thy hands"
Psalm 95:1—"O come, let us sing for joy to the LORD"
Psalm 96:1—"Sing to the LORD a new song; Sing to the LORD, all the earth"
Psalm 96:2—"Sing to the LORD, bless His name"

Psalm 98:1—"O sing to the LORD a new song"
Psalm 98:4—"Break forth and sing for joy and sing
 praises"
Psalm 100:2—"Come before Him with joyful
 singing"
Psalm 108:1—"My heart is steadfast, O God; I will
 sing, I will sing praises, even with my soul"
Psalm 147:7—"Sing to the LORD with thanksgiving"
Psalm 149:1—"Sing to the LORD a new song"

Obviously, music is an essential in worship (no matter whether you sing on key or not). The Christian church should be a singing church: congregational singing, choral singing, individuals singing, all of us praising God with songs.

What About Musical Instruments?

A few religious groups say that musical instruments should not be used in worship. But the biblical evidence to the contrary is overwhelming (Ps. 81:2; 87:7; 92:3; 98:5-6; 108:2; 144:9; 147:7; 149:3).

Praise Him with trumpet sound;
Praise Him with harp and lyre.
Praise Him with timbrel and dancing;
Praise Him with stringed instruments and pipe.
Praise Him with loud cymbals;
Praise Him with resounding cymbals.
Let everything that has breath praise the LORD.
Praise the LORD!

(Ps. 150:3-6)

We see that all kinds of instruments can be used, and the level of noise is often encouraged to be "loud." That idea might shock those who would insist on the music of God's people being soft and quiet. That's not what the Scriptures teach. Joyful

133

singing, shouting, and loud instruments are all encouraged in the praise and worship of our Lord.

3. *Giving.* Giving our offerings to God is an act of worship, not a "necessary evil" to keep the church functioning during the week. We don't give (or shouldn't) because the church needs money—although that is certainly true. We give in order to worship and praise the Lord. If this motivation would begin to capture our hearts, there would be less need for emotional pleas for money. We ought to be excited about the privilege of bringing our offerings to God.

Paul wrote about that kind of giving. "Let each one do just as he has purposed in his heart; not grudgingly or under compulsion; for God loves a cheerful giver" (2 Cor. 9:7). The word for "cheerful" in that verse is related to our English word "hilarity." Christian giving should be characterized by joy.

The spirit of worshipful giving was expressed like this by David. "Now therefore, our God, we thank Thee, and praise Thy glorious name. But who am I and who are my people that we should be able to offer as generously as this? For all things come from Thee, and from Thy hand we have given Thee" (1 Chron. 29:13-14).

Earlier in that chapter we read: "Then the people rejoiced because they had offered so willingly, for they made their offering to the LORD with a whole heart, and King David also rejoiced greatly" (v. 9).

Do we give willingly to God, expressing by that act our thanks to Him? Giving is an act of worship.

4. *Preaching and Teaching.* The preaching and

teaching of God's Word should encourage our hearts to worship God. It honors Him when we open His Word and desire to hear what He wants of us. Explaining what the Bible says and means is an act of worship (cf. Neh. 8:5-8). Paul told Timothy, "Until I come, give attention to the public reading of Scripture, to exhortation and teaching" (1 Tim. 4:13).

5. *Communion*. The taking of the Bread and the Cup is a special act of worship. It remembers the Lord's death until He comes. It is the Christian Passover and Feast of Unleavened Bread (1 Cor. 5:7). It is the symbol of the New Covenant of God promised in Jeremiah 31:31-34, the promise of sins forgiven. Concerning the Bread of the Passover meal, Jesus said, "Take, eat; this is My body" and "Drink from it, all of you; for this is My blood of the covenant, which is to be shed on behalf of many for forgiveness of sins" (Mt. 26:26-28).

Paul taught:

> For I received from the Lord that which I also delivered to you, that the Lord Jesus in the night in which He was betrayed took bread; and when He had given thanks, He broke it, and said, "This is My body, which is for you; do this in remembrance of Me." In the same way He took the cup also, after supper, saying, "This cup is the new covenant in My blood; do this, as often as you drink it, in remembrance of Me." For as often as you eat this bread and drink the cup, you proclaim the Lord's death until He comes (1 Cor. 11:23-26).

And, "Is not the cup of blessing which we bless a sharing in the blood of Christ? Is not the bread which we break a sharing in the body of Christ?"

135

(1 Cor. 10:16). The questions assume a "yes" answer. Those symbols are intended to remind us of our Savior's work of redemption.

Though forms and ceremonies change from one generation to another, these acts of worship remain essential for believers: prayer, music, giving, preaching and teaching, communion. How they are put into practice is a question for each generation and each church to decide.

The key word to guide us might be the word *celebration*. We are celebrating the Person and work of God Almighty when we come to worship as a corporate body of people. In *Worship: Rediscovering the Missing Jewel*, by Ronald Allen and Gordon Borror (Multnomah Press), we have these words:

> What, then, is the essence of worship? It is the celebration of God! When we worship God, we celebrate Him: We extol Him, we sound His praises, we boast in Him.
>
> Worship is not the casual chatter that occasionally drowns out the organ prelude; we celebrate God when we allow the prelude to attune our hearts to the glory of God by the means of the music.
>
> Worship is not the mumbling of prayers or the mouthing of hymns with little thought and less heart; we celebrate God when we join together earnestly in prayer and intensely in song.
>
> Worship is not self-aggrandizing words or boring cliches when one is asked to give a testimony; we celebrate God when we boast in His name to the good of His people.
>
> Worship is not irrelevant thoughts or fragmented elements, silly asides or unconnected directions in purpose; we celebrate God when all of the parts of the service fit together and work to a com-

mon end.

Worship is not grudging gifts or compulsory service; we celebrate God when we give to Him hilariously and serve Him with integrity.

Worship is not haphazard music done poorly, not even great music done merely as a performance; we celebrate God when we enjoy and participate in music to His glory.

Worship is not a distracted endurance of the sermon; we celebrate God as we hear His Word gladly and seek to be conformed by it more and more to the image of our Savior.

Worship is not a sermon that is poorly prepared and carelessly delivered; we celebrate God when we honor His Word with our words, by His Spirit.

Worship is not the hurried motions of a "tacked-on" Lord's Table; we celebrate God pre-eminently when we fellowship gratefully at the ceremonial meal that speaks so centrally of our faith in the Christ Who died for us, Who rose again on our behalf, and Who is to return for our good.

As a thoughtful gift is a celebration of a birthday, as a special evening out is a celebration of an anniversary, as a warm eulogy is a celebration of a life, as a sexual embrace is a celebration of a marriage— so a worship service is a celebration of God. (pp. 18-19).

For those tremendous words, I have this worshipful response: Amen. On second thought, make that AMEN (said with a shout!).

A Place to Begin

What does worship mean to you? Do you worship God daily, or is your worship limited to one hour on Sunday morning?

Try to put into your own words who God is.

137

What has He done in your life that should elicit your worship?

Prayer is essential in our worship of God. What present concerns need to be undergirded by your prayer? Are you a man or woman of prayer? Do you desire to be?

Have you learned to give to others as an act of worship? Who needs your help right now?

HOW DO WE PLEASE GOD?

1. By EXALTING Jesus Christ, His Son.
   Matthew 3:17; Colossians 1:15-19

2. By PROCLAIMING the message of the cross.
   1 Corinthians 1:18–2:5

3. By BELIEVING in God and His promises.
   Hebrews 11:6

4. By ASKING for wisdom.
   1 Kings 3:10; Colossians 1:9-14; James 1:5-8

5. By STAYING AWAY from sexual sin.
   Ephesians 5:3,4,10; 1 Thessalonians 4:1-8

6. By SHARING the gospel with unbelievers.
   1 Corinthians 9:15-27; 10:31-33

7. By GIVING to others in time of need.
   Philippians 4:10-20; Hebrews 13:16

8. By SUBMITTING to authority.
   Romans 8:7,8; Colossians 3:20; 1 John 3:22

9. By PRAISING God for all things.
   Psalm 69:30,31; Hebrews 13:15,16